NO PRICES NO GAMES!
FOUR ECONOMIC MODELS

NO PRICES NO GAMES!
FOUR ECONOMIC MODELS

Michael Richter

Baruch College
Royal Holloway, University of London

Ariel Rubinstein

Tel Aviv University
New York University

OpenBook
Publishers

ISBN Paperback: 978-1-80511-308-9
ISBN Hardback: 978-1-80511-309-6
ISBN Digital (PDF): 978-1-80511-310-2
DOI: 10.11647/OBP.0404

Cover image: Ariel Rubinstein
Cover concept: Michael Richter and Ariel Rubinstein
Cover design: Jeevanjot Kaur Nagpal

Contents

Personal Note   vii

Notation and Terminology   ix

0   Introduction   1
   0.1   The Book   1
   0.2   The Notion of an Economy   3
   0.3   Examples of Economies   4
   0.4   Equilibrium Concepts   8

1   Equilibrium in the Jungle   13
   1.1   The Housing Jungle: Model and Equilibrium   15
   1.2   The Jungle Equilibrium: Welfare   18
   1.3   Comparison to the Competitive Equilibrium   21
   1.4   Comments on the Jungle Equilibrium   25
   1.5   The Division Jungle   28
   1.6   The Division Jungle: Comments on Welfare   33
   1.7   A Didactic Perspective   34

2   The Permissible and the Forbidden   37
   2.1   The Y-Equilibrium Concept   39
   2.2   Y-Equilibrium, Pareto Optimality, and Envy-Freeness   43
   2.3   Euclidean Economies   45
   2.4   The "Kosher" Economy   46
   2.5   Convex Y-Equilibrium   49
   2.6   Pareto Optimality and Existence of Convex Y-Equilibrium   51
   2.7   A Structure Theorem for Convex Y-equilibrium   53
   2.8   The Division Economy   55
   2.9   The Give-and-Take Economy   59
   2.10   The Stay Close Economy   61

3   Status and Indoctrination   65

   3.1   Status Equilibrium   67

   3.2   Status Equilibrium – Examples   68

   3.3   A Detour: Convex Preferences   71

   3.4   Primitive Equilibrium   76

   3.5   A First Welfare Theorem   79

   3.6   A Second Welfare Theorem   81

   3.7   Primitive Equilibrium – Examples   83

   3.8   Initial Status Equilibrium   85

4   Biased Preferences Equilibrium   91

   4.1   The Economy and the Equilibrium Concept   92

   4.2   The Give-and-Take Economy   98

   4.3   The Fixed-Prices Exchange Economy   100

   4.4   Housing-Type Economies   104

5   A Comparison to Game Theory   111

   5.1   The Matching Economy   112

   5.2   The Jungle Equilibrium   115

   5.3   Restricting Partnerships: Pairwise Y-equilibrium   120

   5.4   Prestige by Partner: Status Equilibrium   122

   5.5   Prestige by Self: Initial Status Equilibrium   124

   5.6   A Comparison of Approaches   127

   5.7   The Majority Voting Economy   127

   5.8   Convex Y-equilibrium   128

   5.9   Biased Preferences Equilibrium   130

   5.10   The Majority Voting Game and Nash Equilibrium   131

   5.11   Comparing our Approaches with Nash Equilibrium   133

References   134

Personal Note

We feel some dissatisfaction with current trends in Economic Theory. Novelty has fallen by the wayside. Models have become overly complicated and excessively sophisticated mathematically. Papers are too long and contain few new fundamental ideas. Authors go to great lengths to masquerade theoretical work as being applied.

This book contains a collection of models in Economic Theory that are simple in their approach and straightforward mathematically. They include new concepts and are presented concisely, without any pretend claims regarding their direct applied usefulness. At best, the models have helped us to understand various social institutions, such as power, status, social norms, and preference biases as a means to achieve harmony in economic environments. Needless to say, we do not advocate for the adoption of any of these institutions but, rather, investigate their rationales. Our main objective is to disrupt the convention that every economic model should be either a market with prices or a strategic game.

This project began just over a decade ago and developed from a series of papers, most of which we wrote jointly. The book brings the papers together in a unified language and an accessible style. It can be used to teach a unit in an advanced Economic Theory course or as a source for independent study.

We wish to acknowledge generous assistance from two outstanding individuals: Martin Osborne, who was kind, as always, and shared with us the format of the book which he originally designed (so, if you are happy with the format, you should thank him) and Áron Tóbiás, who contributed so much of his time to carefully reviewing a draft of the book and saved us (and you) from a large number of errors. We are also grateful to Tuval Danenberg for his comments.

MR: I am grateful to the support of my wife, Emel Yildirim-Richter, without whom this project would never have been completed.

URLs: https://mrichter.co and https://arielrubinstein.tau.ac.il

Notation and Terminology

While the the book uses standard notation, we emphasize the following notational conventions:

Superscripts: A *superscript* always indicates an agent. For example, x^i is the choice of agent i and $\succsim^i$ is his preference relation.

Subscripts: A *subscript* is used for all other indices. In particular, when an element x is a member of some Euclidean space, then x_k denotes the kth component of the vector x.

Profile: The notation $(x^i)_{i \in N}$ indicates a *profile* of choices, one for each agent $i \in N$. Often, we omit the subscript "$i \in N$" and will simply use the notation (x^i). Given a set Y, the set Y^N is the set of all possible profiles of choices from Y.

Ordering: An *ordering* is a binary relation on a set that satisfies reflexivity, completeness, and transitivity. A *strict ordering* is an ordering that is antisymmetric (that is, it has no indifferences). An agent i's ordering is denoted by $\succsim^i$. The expression $x \succsim^i y$ means that "agent i weakly prefers x to y" and $x \succ^i y$ means that "agent i strictly prefers x to y".

Pareto Dominance: Let $(\succsim^i)_{i \in N}$ be a profile of orderings on a set Y. The profile $(a^i) \in Y^N$ *Pareto-dominates* the vector $(b^i) \in Y^N$ if $a^i \succsim^i b^i$ for all $i \in N$ with at least one strict inequality. Given any subset of Y^N, we say that a profile (a^i) is *Pareto-optimal* in that subset if it does not contain any other profile that Pareto-dominates (a^i).

0 Introduction

0.1 The Book

We regard Economic Theory as a collection of models, each viewed as a story or a fable rather than as a testable scientific model to be verified or refuted (see Rubinstein (2012)). Models in Economic Theory are "useful" in the same sense that fables are. Perhaps, there is no boy who literally "cried wolf", but we nevertheless tell the story to teach our children about the dangers of exaggeration. Likewise, the fables we tell in Economic Theory are not meant to be "true" but, rather, are intended to draw our attention to some aspect of real economic life. We view the construction and analysis of models in Economic Theory as a cultural endeavour rather than a scientific one.

Almost all models of interaction between agents in current Economic Theory belong to one of two families: Markets or Games. In market models, there are conflicts over limited resources that are resolved through the emergence of prices, which are taken as given by the agents. These prices bring order to the economic chaos by orchestrating the behaviour of selfish agents. In game-theoretical models, each agent (player) chooses a strategy, and an equilibrium is a profile of strategies such that each agent's strategy is individually optimal, given the correct prediction of other players' behavior. In other words, in a market, each agent chooses his best alternative given the prevailing prices, while in a game, each agent chooses his best strategy based on correct forecasts of what other agents intend to do.

While market models dominated Economic Theory for most of the 20th century, Game Theory subsequently captured the crown. In the last few decades, Economic Theory has seen another change: economic theorists have liberated themselves from the rigid assumption of full rationality in the pursuit of materialistic goals. The Bounded Rationality literature replaced the

  https://doi.org/10.11647/OBP.0404.00

rationality assumption with explicit reference to decision procedures, while the Behavioral Economics literature added realistic psychological motives to purely materialistic considerations. However, these developments left in place the standard view of economic interactions as being resolved through prices or games.

This short book is aimed primarily at young economists. It is intended to demonstrate models of interaction between agents with NO PRICES and NO GAMES. We do not claim that these models are any more (or less) "true", "realistic", or "useful" than others. In fact, we do not believe that these adjectives are even relevant to models in Economic Theory. As mentioned, we view these models as economic stories: they are interesting; they capture some aspect of reality; they are elegant; they are novel; or ... not.

In the models we study, agents are purely self-interested, and equilibrium reflects a social institution that systematically alters either the agents' choice sets or their preferences. In this respect, the models are closer to market models than to game-theoretical models, and, as in the case of market models, an equilibrium will not be just a profile of choices made by individuals, but will also specify an additional price-like element that uniformly affects all agents.

While we do not have any applied message, working on these topics has brought us to the realization that economic harmony can be achieved by institutions other than prices or games. Of course, this realization could have happened even without any models, but they illuminate how such institutions may function in bringing harmony to economic situations. We focus on four institutions: *Power* (Chapter 1), *Social Norms governing what is permissible and what is forbidden* (Chapter 2), *Status* (Chapter 3), and *Preference Biases* (Chapter 4). In the last part of the book (Chapter 5), we compare our approach to other more established ones. We refrain from any normative assessments of the institutions. Such judgements are left to the reader.

0.2   The Notion of an Economy

The stage on which this book's plots will be performed is a formal model called an *economy*. The model is intended to abstractly capture situations in which each agent in a society chooses an alternative and there exists a fundamental tension between the agents' personal desires and society-wide feasibility constraints. (For example, in a Walrasian economy, consumers have unquenchable desires, but overall resources are limited.) The model's abstraction allows us to consider examples that are "economics" in the conventional sense of the term, but also others that are not. Nevertheless, the term "economy" will be used throughout since all of the models feature the fundamental economic conundrum: individuals' desires cannot all be satisfied due to feasibility constraints on the profiles of choices that can be made in the society.

Definition: Economy

An **economy** is a tuple $\langle N, X, (\succsim^i)_{i \in N}, F \rangle$ where:

- $N = \{1, \ldots, n\}$ is the set of agents.

- X is a set of personal alternatives.
  Each agent chooses an *element* from X. In its most general form, no structure is imposed on X; however, we sometimes consider the special case where X is a subset of a Euclidean space.

- $\succsim^i$ is agent i's preference relation over the set X.
  The fact that preferences are defined over X rather than over the set of choice profiles embodies the assumption that there are no externalities: each agent cares *only* about his chosen alternative irrespective of what other agents choose (as in the case of markets, but unlike in the case of games).

- $F \subset X^N$ is a non-empty set of feasible profiles.

  A choice profile $(x^i)_{i \in N}$ specifies an element $x^i \in X$ for each agent $i \in N$. The set X^N is comprised of all choice profiles. Not all profiles are feasible, and the feasibility constraint is given by a set $F \subset X^N$. Unless stated otherwise, we assume that F is closed under all permutations (i.e. the feasibility constraint is anonymous and does not discriminate between agents). We usually abbreviate $(x^i)_{i \in N}$ as (x^i).

An economy without preferences, $\langle N, X, F \rangle$, is called an **environment**.

Sometimes, we consider an extended version of an economy which specifies for each agent i an element e^i in X, with the interpretation that i always has the right to choose e^i. The vector (e^i) is required to be in F, namely the allocation of these initial rights is feasible. The role of the vector (e^i) is analogous to that of the profile of initial endowments in the standard exchange economy.

Definition: Extended Economy

An **extended economy** is a tuple $\langle N, X, (\succsim^i)_{i \in N}, F, (e^i)_{i \in N} \rangle$ where:

- $\langle N, X, (\succsim^i)_{i \in N}, F \rangle$ is an economy.

- $(e^i)_{i \in N}$ is a feasible initial profile.

0.3   Examples of Economies

We now introduce some economies which appear throughout the book. As mentioned, some of the examples are traditional economic settings while others demonstrate the framework's ability to model a variety of alternative social situations.

Example: The Housing Economy

The set X contains n distinct elements called *houses* (recall that n is the number of agents) and each agent i has preferences $\succsim^i$ over the houses. Each agent chooses a house, but no two agents can occupy the same one. That is, F is the set of profiles that assigns a distinct house to every agent. This economy is the iconic model of Shapley and Scarf (1974). The model is attractive due to its simplicity and its usefulness as a platform for introducing a rich variety of concepts.

If each agent's ideal is distinct, then the situation is "bliss", there are no conflicting desires, and so there is no need for a social institution to achieve harmony in the society. However, bliss does not usually exist, and, therefore, we need social institutions to resolve the conflict between agents' desires and societal feasibility.

Example: The Division Economy

There are K commodities, and the set of alternatives $X = \mathbb{R}_+^K$ consists of the non-negative bundles of those commodities. Preference relations are monotonic, continuous, and convex. As in standard market settings, there are limited resources, and the set of feasible profiles $F = \{(x^i) \mid \Sigma_i x^i = e\}$ is the set of all partitions of a total endowment $e \in \mathbb{R}_+^K$ among the agents. If we would add initial endowments to the model, then we would obtain the classical framework used by economists since Edgeworth (1881) to discuss voluntary exchange and competitive equilibrium. Bliss is always impossible, unlimited wants must be constrained in the face of limited resources, and achieving social harmony requires some social institution.

Example: The Give-and-Take Economy

There are situations in life in which redistribution is imposed by an authority that forces individuals to comply, and there are others in which redistribution is accomplished by means of voluntary exchange between individuals. There are further situations (e.g. a soup kitchen) in which exchange is carried out by unilateral actions: some individuals give while others take without any exercise of power, commitments to "return the favour", or coercion by an authority. These actions are self-motivated: some people like to give, while others like to take. But typically, such motives will not balance each other out, and social norms are needed to achieve harmony.

Formally, we consider the following give-and-take economy, which was first studied by Sprumont (1991). Let $X = [-1, 1]$, where a positive x represents a withdrawal of x from a social fund (i.e. taking) and a negative x represents a contribution of $|x|$ to the social fund (i.e. giving). Preferences are assumed to be continuous and strictly convex (that is, single-peaked) but need not be monotonic. Feasibility requires that the social fund is balanced, that is, $F = \{(x^i) \mid \Sigma_i x^i = 0\}$.

Example: The Clubs Economy

The set X consists of a finite set of clubs (see Buchanan (1965)). Each agent chooses a single club to become a member of. Agents have preferences over the clubs and not over the clubs' members. The feasibility constraint is defined by the limits on how many people can belong to each club. Specifically, there is a vector of positive integers $(q_x)_{x \in X}$ where q_x is the quota for club x (for non-triviality, we require that the sum of the quotas is at least n). The set of feasible profiles are those for which no club is chosen by more people than allowed by its capacity.

Example: The Stay Close Economy

This example illustrates the potential of our abstract concept to expand the scope of classical economic analysis. It does not involve goods but nonetheless fits squarely into our concept of an economy. In this example, X is a set of locations in some geographical area. Each agent chooses a location in X and has preferences over the locations. Not every profile of locations is feasible because the society is under threat and its survival depends upon the ability of its members to quickly reach one another in the case of danger. Therefore, all members need to live close enough to each other so that whenever one of them is attacked the others can quickly come to his defence. Formally, the feasibility constraint F requires that the distance between any two agents does not exceed some constant d. When d is very large, every agent can choose his ideal location, but when d is small, this is no longer feasible.

We refer to the special case when $d = 0$ as the *consensus economy*. This fits, for example, the situation of a political party whose members need to present a united front. That is, in order to maintain cohesion, all members of the party need to express the same position.

Example: The Matching Economy

Matching problems are classics of Cooperative Game Theory. Agents have to find a match, and each agent has a preference relation over his potential partners. This situation fits our framework by letting the set of alternatives X be the set of agents N. That is, each agent chooses a partner, which can be himself. Each has a preference relation on X that places himself at the bottom. The feasibility constraint F stipulates that for any i and j, if i chooses j, then j must choose i. Note that this feasibility constraint differs from those in the previous examples in that F is not closed under all permutations.

> ### Example: The Sequential Production Economy
>
> A group of n agents works in n shifts to transform an initial product x^0 into a different product. Each works one shift, and the agents may work in any order. An agent's ability to produce a product, which might be just an intermediate product, depends on the output of the previous shift. The group possesses a technology that enables certain transformations of one product into another.
>
> More precisely, X is a set of products that includes x^0. Each agent has preferences for the product that he produces (rather than for the final product). The common production technology is a correspondence T from X to X where $T(x)$ is the set of outputs which x can be transformed into. Any agent can choose to be "idle" and not transform the product produced in the previous shift, that is $x \in T(x)$. Thus, F is the set of all permutations of profiles $(x^1, \ldots, x^n)$ such that $x^m \in T(x^{m-1})$ for $m = 1, \ldots, n$.

0.4   Equilibrium Concepts

This book introduces and analyzes several solution concepts and applies them to a variety of economic environments. In general, a solution concept relates to some domain of economic environments and determines for each environment a set of harmonious outcomes. These outcomes are harmonious in the sense that the assumed forces that may disturb harmony are neutralized. In our setting, the domain of a solution concept is a class of economies and a candidate for equilibrium typically includes two components:

(i) **A profile of choices** — one choice for each agent.

(ii) A specification of certain **parameters** that systematically influence either agents' choice problems or their preference relations.

Harmony is achieved in equilibrium as follows: agents make individually optimal choices, and the parameters restrict their choice sets (or, in one case, biases their preferences) to be compatible in the sense that the resulting profile of choices is feasible. The concepts will differ in the parameters and in how they restrict agents' choice sets.

The solution concepts discussed in the book can be divided into two groups. In the **choice group**, each agent's choice set depends on a price-like equilibrium parameter but not on the equilibrium profile of choices. Such choices must be individually optimal and compatible. These concepts are similar in structure to the notion of competitive equilibrium whose parameters are prices and each agent's choice set (budget set) is determined solely by his initial endowment and the prices.

Three of our solution concepts belong to this group:

Y-equilibrium (Chapter 2). The price-like parameter in a Y-equilibrium is a set of alternatives which is interpreted as the set of "permissible" alternatives that uniformly binds all agents. When making a choice, an agent only needs to know the set of permissible alternatives and nothing else. In equilibrium, the permissible set is a maximal set of alternatives from among those which satisfy the following property: if every agent chooses a preference-maximizing alternative from this set, then the resulting choice profile is feasible.

Initial Status Equilibrium (Chapter 3). This concept relates to an extended economy wherein the notion of an economy is enriched with an additional element: a feasible profile of alternatives, one for each agent, in which the alternative designated to an agent is interpreted as one that he always has the right to choose. The price-like parameter in an initial status equilibrium is an ordering of the alternatives that can be interpreted as "status" or "value". An agent's choice set is comprised of all alternatives which have a weakly lower status than his endowment. In equilibrium, a status ordering prevails such that each agent's designated alternative is his most preferred from among his choice set, namely the set of all alternatives that are of weakly lower status than his initial alternative. As always, an equilibrium profile of choices has to be feasible.

Biased Preferences Equilibrium (Chapter 4). The price-like parameter in a biased preferences equilibrium is a vector that systematically biases agents' preferences. In this model, agents' choice sets are fixed and unaffected by the parameters. Rather, in an equilibrium, a systematic bias prevails such that each agent chooses a most-preferred alternative from his choice set, according to his biased preferences, and the profile of choices is feasible.

In the **deviation group** of solution concepts, an equilibrium is a profile of choices that is immune to any single agent's deviation from his prescribed alternative to any alternative in a set determined by the equilibrium parameters. This is the approach taken in Game Theory. For example, a Nash equilibrium is a profile of actions such that, for each agent, the outcome of that profile is not worse for him than any other outcome he can achieve given the other players' choices in the profile.

Two of our solution concepts fall into this group:

Jungle Equilibrium (Chapter 1). In this case, the economy is extended with an exogenous power ranking of the agents; but, in an equilibrium, there are no additional parameters. In the jungle, an agent can steal from those that are weaker than himself; therefore, his choice set is determined by his equilibrium choice as well as the choices of those who are weaker than him. A jungle equilibrium is a profile of choices such that each agent's assigned choice is preference-maximal from among the set of the alternatives he can obtain by stealing resources from weaker agents.

Status Equilibrium (Chapter 3). Again, the price-like equilibrium parameter is an ordering over the alternatives that connotes status (or value). However, in this case, an agent's choice set depends not only on this parameter but also on his own equilibrium alternative. In detail, his choice set is the set of all alternatives which are weakly lower-ranked than his *equilibrium alternative* (rather than his initial alternative). An equilibrium is a status ordering and a profile of optimal choices such that the profile of choices is feasible.

The book analyzes each of these solution concepts both in the abstract, by means of general propositions, and more concretely, by applying the solution concepts to a variety of economic environments (some familiar and some novel).

1 Equilibrium in the Jungle

The standard economic approach treats economic activity as voluntary: all involved parties are doing whatever they do of their own free will. When analyzed using the competitive equilibrium approach, economic agents operate within bounds set by a price system that they take as given, but their decisions are free — no one forces them to act. When analyzed using the game-theoretical approach, agents behave strategically, and in equilibrium they best respond to correct predictions about the other agents' behavior, and, again, no one can force anyone to take a particular action.

However, life is not just a series of voluntary actions. An agent (or a group of agents) might use power to seize assets from others or to force others to do things against their will. Resources are often transferred from one agent to another based on the exercise of power, rather than due to the satisfaction of mutual wants. While an agent can use power to force another to behave against his best interests, there is often no need to actually use power since the mere threat of doing so can be sufficient to persuade a weaker agent to give in.

Economic Theory typically ignores the use of power as a driver of social activity. In the words of Hirshleifer (1994) (see also Bowles and Gintis (1992) and Grossman (1995) who express similar sentiments):

> … the mainline Marshallian tradition has … almost entirely overlooked what I will call the dark side of the force — to wit, crime, war, and politics. … Appropriating, grabbing, confiscating what you want — and, on the flip side, defending, protecting, sequestering what you already have — that's economic activity too.

As the title of the book promises, we consider economic interactions that are harmonized without the emergence of a price system or the use of strategic

  https://doi.org/10.11647/OBP.0404.01

deliberation. In this chapter, we shine a spotlight on the use of power by presenting a model where a power relation between the agents together with their preferences determine the outcome of their economic interactions.

The first notion of power that comes to mind is brute force. But power takes many softer forms. For example, power based on rank and seniority plays an important role in the allocation of resources, and the power of rhetoric or charm often allows one person to convince another to perform some action.

This chapter closely follows Piccione and Rubinstein (2007) which introduces and analyzes an elementary model of a society referred to as the *jungle*, in which economic transactions are governed only by coercion. The model consists of a set of agents with exogenous preferences over a set of assets and a power ordering of the agents. The ordering is unambiguous and known to all. Power means that a stronger agent is able to take things away from a weaker agent without the weaker agent's consent.

The jungle model is designed to mirror the standard model of an exchange economy. In both models, agents have preferences over assets and the total stock of assets is given. The distribution of power in the jungle replaces the initial distribution of assets in the market. Just as the acquisition of initial endowments is ignored in an exchange economy model, so is the acquisition of power ignored in the jungle model.

The jungle model makes no reference to property rights. An individual holds assets rather than owning them. There is no legal system that protects an individual's assets. Rather, a weaker agent can be forced to give up assets or coerced into an unfavourable exchange by a stronger agent. These features are in contrast to the standard exchange economy where property rights are perfectly enforced and exchanges are carried out only by mutual consent.

The solution concept we employ is called the *jungle equilibrium*. It is a feasible allocation of the assets such that no agent wishes to take assets from an agent (or agents) weaker than himself. In this chapter, we will apply versions of the concept to two different economies. The first is a version of Shapley and Scarf (1974)'s housing economy in which the set of assets is a discrete set of houses where each house can be occupied by only one agent and each agent can hold only one house. The second is the division economy where a bundle of divisible goods is allocated among the agents. Throughout, we will deal with standard issues, such as existence, uniqueness, and the two fundamental theorems of welfare.

1.1 The Housing Jungle: Model and Equilibrium

Recall that the housing economy is a tuple $\langle N, X, (\succsim^i)_{i \in N}, F \rangle$ where N is a finite set of n agents, X is a set of n houses, each agent $i \in N$ has a strict preference relation $\succsim^i$ over X (there are no indifferences), and F is the set of feasible profiles, which consists of all profiles $(x^i) \in X^N$ such that $x^i \neq x^j$ for every two agents i and j. This definition of F stipulates that every agent occupies exactly one house and every house is occupied by exactly one agent.

Note again that in this economy and throughout the book, there are no externalities in preferences (as in the standard market model). Each agent's preferences are defined over X, that is, an agent only cares about his own house and not about who occupies the others.

The jungle model's key ingredient is a power relation $\triangleright$, which is a strict ordering (complete, asymmetric, and transitive) on the set of individuals. The term $i \triangleright j$ is read as "agent i is stronger than agent j", which means that i can confiscate any house occupied by j. In summary,

---

Definition: Jungle Housing Economy

A **jungle housing economy** is a tuple $\langle N, X, (\succsim^i)_{i \in N}, F, \triangleright \rangle$ where:

- $N = \{1, \ldots, n\}$ is the set of agents.
- X is the set of houses and $|X| = n$.
- $\succsim^i$ is agent i's strict ordering over the houses.
- F is the set of all profiles $(x^i)_{i \in N}$ such that $x^i \neq x^j$ for any two agents i, j.
- The *power relation* $\triangleright$ is a strict ordering on the set of agents N. Without loss of generality, we assume that $1 \triangleright 2 \triangleright \cdots \triangleright n$.

Comments on the notion of power

The power relation is exogenous: The model does not specify the source of power. As mentioned earlier, this is analogous to market settings where the initial endowments are taken as given without specifying their source. Naturally, one can think about models (not discussed here) in which the attainment of power (or initial endowments) is also a part of the model.

The exercise of power does not involve a loss of resources: We have in mind that an agent i who prefers a house currently occupied by a weaker agent j can confiscate it at no cost: i simply presents himself at j's door and j, recognizing his relative weakness, will move out. This is analogous to the standard exchange model where the exercise of trade and the enforcement of property rights are costless.

Power is exercised by an individual, not by a group: A stronger agent can force a weaker one to take an action, but a group of agents cannot form a coalition in order to force some action on another agent. Nor can the defendant then form a rival coalition. This is analogous to the standard exchange economy setting where agents act individually and coalitions cannot be formed (for example, for the purpose of price manipulation).

The power relation is transitive: One can think of situations in which it is not. For example, suppose that there are three components of power: agility, speed, and strength, and one agent can defeat another by being superior in a majority of them. A Condorcet-like configuration is possible where agent 1 is superior to agent 2 in agility and speed, agent 2 is superior to agent 3 in speed and strength, and agent 3 is superior to agent 1 in agility and strength. Thus, $1 \rhd 2 \rhd 3 \rhd 1$.

The outcome of a confrontation is deterministic: If i is stronger than j, then both are aware that, in any contest between them, i will win with certainty. However, uncertainty about the outcome of a confrontation is also plausible. One could think of a model where the power relation is replaced with a function that specifies for each pair of agents the probability of each of them winning a confrontation between them.

A jungle equilibrium is a profile of choices that is stable given the forces at play. In the jungle housing economy, there are two forces which can lead to instability. First, an agent prefers a house that is occupied by a weaker agent. Second, two individuals intend to occupy the same house. Formally:

> **Definition: Jungle Equilibrium**
>
> A **jungle equilibrium** for a jungle housing economy is a profile of houses (x^i) such that:
>
> (i) There are no two agents $i, j \in N$ for which $i \rhd j$ and $x^j \succ^i x^i$.
>
> (ii) The profile (x^i) is in F.

We start our investigation with an existence result:

> **Proposition 1.1: Existence of a Jungle Equilibrium**
>
> Every jungle housing economy has a jungle equilibrium.

> **Proof:**
>
> Let $\langle N, X, (\succsim^i)_{i \in N}, F, \rhd \rangle$ be a jungle housing economy. Recall that the agents are ordered by power, $1 \rhd 2 \rhd \cdots \rhd n$. Existence is shown using the *serial dictatorship* procedure: Agent 1 is assigned his favourite house $x^1 \in X$; agent 2 is assigned his favourite house from among the remaining houses, $x^2 \in X - \{x^1\}$; and successively, each agent, in order of power, is assigned his favourite house from among those remaining after houses have been assigned to all agents stronger than him. Since the number of houses equals the number of agents, the procedure assigns a house to every agent. Furthermore, the procedure assigns every house only once and thus the profile (x^i) is in F. The profile is a jungle equilibrium because for every i the house x^i is the $\succsim^i$-best among all the houses that are possessed by agents not stronger than him.

Note that the serial dictatorship procedure used in the proof is not the equilibrium concept itself but, rather, is a simple algorithm used to prove that an equilibrium exists. Proposition 1.1 above leaves open the possibility that other equilibria may exist. However, we will now show that, given the assumption that all preference relations are strict, the equilibrium is unique.

Proposition 1.2: Uniqueness

Every jungle housing economy has a unique equilibrium.

Proof:

Consider the jungle housing economy $\langle N, X, (\succsim^i)_{i \in N}, F, \triangleright \rangle$. Assume, contrary to the claim, that (a^i) and (b^i) are two different equilibria of the jungle. Denote by i^* the strongest individual i for whom $a^i \neq b^i$. Suppose that $a^{i^*} \succ^{i^*} b^{i^*}$. Since the set of houses allocated to individuals 1 through $i^* - 1$ is the same in both (a^i) and (b^i), it must be that in (b^i), the house a^{i^*} is held by an agent j who is weaker than i^*. Thus, $i^* \triangleright j$ and $b^j = a^{i^*} \succ^{i^*} b^{i^*}$ which contradicts (b^i) being an equilibrium.

1.2   The Jungle Equilibrium: Welfare

We move to discuss two fundamental welfare theorems. In abstract, the first states that, for any initial conditions, equilibrium outcomes are Pareto-optimal profiles; while the second states that Pareto-optimal profiles are equilibrium outcomes for some initial conditions. In the jungle housing economy, the initial condition is the power relation. We now bring proofs of the fundamental welfare theorems for the jungle housing economy (Abdulkadıroğlu and Sönmez (1998) show equivalent results that the set of allocations obtained by a serial dictatorship of some order is equal to the set of Pareto-optimal allocations).

Proposition 1.3: The First Welfare Theorem

The jungle equilibrium is Pareto optimal.

Proof:

Recall the assumption that preferences are strict. Let (x^i) be the jungle equilibrium. Assume that, contrary to the claim, there is a feasible profile (y^i) that Pareto dominates (x^i). Let i be the strongest agent for whom $y^i \neq x^i$. Then, $y^i \succ^i x^i$ and $x^j = y^i$ for some agent j weaker than i, contradicting the fact that (x^i) is a jungle equilibrium.

The above proof relies on the strictness of the agents' preferences. If some individuals have indifferences in their preferences, then a jungle equilibrium might not be Pareto optimal. For example, in the case of two agents and two houses a and b, if $a \sim^1 b$ and $a \succ^2 b$, then both $(x^1, x^2) = (a, b)$ and (b, a) are jungle equilibria, but the profile (a, b) is not Pareto optimal.

We now move to the second welfare theorem. Since the initial conditions for the jungle housing economy are a power relation, the appropriate second welfare theorem states that for any Pareto-optimal profile, there is a power relation for which the jungle equilibrium is precisely that profile. Recall that in the standard exchange model, the social planner assigns initial endowments to the agents with the expectation that trade between them will yield the desired allocation of the total endowment. Analogously, in the jungle housing economy, the social planner assigns the power relation with the expectation that the law of the jungle will yield the desired allocation of the houses.

Proposition 1.4: The Second Welfare Theorem

Given any housing economy $\langle N, X, (\succsim^i)_{i \in N}, F \rangle$ and Pareto-optimal profile (x^i), there exists a power relation $\rhd$ such that (x^i) is the unique jungle equilibrium of the jungle housing economy $\langle N, X, (\succsim^i)_{i \in N}, F, \rhd \rangle$.

Proof:

First, note that in every Pareto-optimal profile (x^i), at least one individual is allocated his favourite house: Otherwise, start with some agent i_0, and define i_{k+1} to be the agent who holds i_k's favourite house ($i_{k+1} \neq i_k$ because no agent's favourite house is his current house). Since N is finite, there will eventually be some l such that $k > l \geq 0$ and $i_{k+1} = i_l$. Then, assigning $y^{i_j} = x^{i_{j+1}}$ for each $l \leq j \leq k$, and keeping $y^j = x^j$ for all other agents, we obtain a feasible allocation (y^i) which Pareto-dominates (x^i).

We construct a power relation $\rhd$ as follows: Let i_1 be an agent for whom x^{i_1} is his first-best house and make him the most powerful agent. Now remove i_1 from the set of individuals and x^{i_1} from the set of houses. The inductive process continues as follows: at the beginning of the $k+1^{\text{st}}$ stage, k agents have been assigned power. The allocation of the remaining houses among the remaining agents is Pareto optimal; therefore, identify an agent i_{k+1} for whom $x^{i_{k+1}}$ is his favourite house from among $X - \{x^{i_1}, \ldots, x^{i_k}\}$ and make him the $(k+1)^{\text{st}}$-most powerful individual.

By construction, for each agent i, the house x^i is preferred by i over every house that is allocated to an individual weaker than him according to $\rhd$. Thus, (x^i) is a jungle equilibrium of $\langle N, X, (\succsim^i)_{i \in N}, F, \rhd \rangle$.

Externalities: To incorporate externalities, we modify the model by defining the agents' preferences over the set of feasible profiles (rather than the set of houses) and by allowing indifferences. The definition of a jungle equilibrium also needs to be modified. When deciding whether to confiscate a house, an agent compares the current profile to the one that would result if he does so. One way to proceed is by interpreting $i \rhd j$ to mean that agent i can force j to exchange houses: i takes over the house occupied by j *and* forces j to accept the house i previously occupied. Thus, an *equilibrium of the jungle with externalities* $\langle N, X, (\succsim^i)_{i \in N}, F, \rhd \rangle$ is a feasible profile (a^i) such that for no two agents $j, j' \in N$ is it the case that $j \rhd j'$ and $(b^i) \succ^j (a^i)$, where (b^i) is the allocation that differs from (a^i) only in the fact that $b^j = a^{j'}$ and $b^{j'} = a^j$.

In the model with externalities, a jungle equilibrium does not necessarily exist. For example, consider a case with 3 agents where $1 \rhd 2 \rhd 3$ and $X = \{a, b, c\}$. Think of the houses as being located clockwise on a circle: $a \to b \to c \to a$. Suppose that agent 1 top-ranks the three profiles where he is the clockwise neighbour of 2. Likewise, agent 2 top-ranks the three profiles where he is the clockwise neighbour of 1. There is no equilibrium because in any profile, agent 3 is the clockwise neighbour of either agent 1 or 2, in which case the other agent desires agent 3's position and is stronger than him. It is also easy to find an example with three individuals in which a jungle equilibrium exists but is not Pareto optimal.

1.3   Comparison to the Competitive Equilibrium

Shapley and Scarf (1974) used the extended housing economy for studying the notion of competitive equilibrium in a simple setting with discrete goods. Recall that the *extended housing economy* is a tuple $\langle N, X, (\succsim^i)_{i \in N}, F, (e^i)_{i \in N} \rangle$ where $\langle N, X, (\succsim^i)_{i \in N}, F \rangle$ is a housing economy and (e^i) is a feasible profile which is interpreted as an initial allocation of the houses. Thus, instead of a power relation, the housing economy model is enriched with the specification of an initial endowment for each agent. Shapley and Scarf (1974) define a *competitive equilibrium* for this extended economy to be a profile of prices (one real number to each house) and a profile of houses such that: (i) each agent prefers his assigned house to any that is not more expensive than his initial endowment and (ii) the housing assignment is feasible. Formally:

Definition: Competitive Equilibrium

A **competitive equilibrium** for an extended housing economy is a tuple $\langle (p_x)_{x \in X}, (x^i)_{i \in N} \rangle$ where $(p_x)_{x \in X}$ is a profile of prices and (x^i) is a profile of houses such that:

(i) For every individual i, the house x^i is $\succsim^i$-maximal in $\{x \mid p_{e^i} \geq p_x\}$.

(ii) The profile (x^i) is in F.

The following proposition, due to Shapley and Scarf (1974), shows that a competitive equilibrium exists. The proof, due to David Gale, uses an algorithm which is based on the notion of a top-trading cycle. Given any group of agents with initial endowments, a *top-trading cycle* is a cycle of agents all of whom most prefer the house of the next agent in the cycle from among those that the group members are endowed with. If an agent prefers his own house to all others then he makes a cycle of length one. We will see that a top-trading cycle always exists.

The top-trading cycle algorithm proceeds as follows: at each stage, a top-trading cycle is identified. Each agent in the cycle is exclusively assigned the house of the next agent in the cycle (which he prefers from among the houses that were not assigned previously). All houses in the cycle are assigned the same price, which is lower than the prices of all previously assigned houses, and both the assigned agents and the assigned houses are removed.

> **Proposition 1.5: Existence of Competitive Equilibrium**
>
> For any extended housing economy, a competitive equilibrium exists.

> **Proof:**
>
> Let $\langle N, X, (\succsim^i)_{i \in N}, F, (e^i)_{i \in N} \rangle$ be an extended housing economy. We first show that a top-trading cycle exists for every group of agents G. Start arbitrarily with an agent $i_0 \in G$, and define $i_{k+1} \in G$ as the initial holder of i_k's favourite house from the set of houses belonging to G. Since the group is finite, there will eventually be some l such that $k \geq l \geq 0$ and $i_{k+1} = i_l$. Then, the sequence $(i_l, \ldots, i_k)$ constitutes a top-trading cycle. See Figure 1.1 for an illustration of the argument where $l = 2$ and $k = 5$.
>
>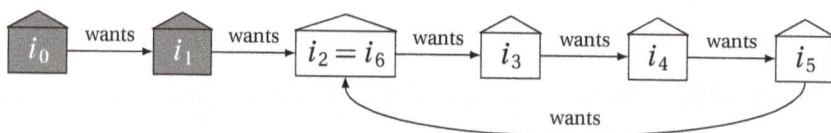
>
> **Figure 1.1** The Top–Trading Cycle algorithm.

The algorithm constructs a partition $\{I_1, \ldots, I_l, \ldots, I_L\}$ of N as follows: First, find a top-trading cycle from the group of all agents. Set I_1 to be the set of members of this cycle and assign to each of them the house he most prefers. Continue inductively: at stage $l+1$, find a top-trading cycle from among the group $N - I_1 - \ldots - I_l$ and for each member of the cycle assign the house which he most prefers from among those initially held by the group. Set I_{l+1} to be the set of members in the cycle. Continue in this fashion until a partition is completed. Choose a sequence of numbers $p_1 > p_2 > \ldots > p_L > 0$ and, for each $x \in X$, define $p_x = p_l$ where the agent who initially occupies x is in I_l. The assigned profile (x^i) together with the price vector (p_x) constitutes a competitive equilibrium because $(x^i) \in F$, and every agent i in I_l chooses his favourite house from within his "budget set", namely the set of houses initially held by the members of $I_l \cup \ldots \cup I_L$.

Comparing the above construction to that of the jungle equilibrium clarifies the source of power in the market vs. the source of power in the jungle. In Gale's construction, in each round some agents obtain their favourite house from among those not allocated in previous rounds. So too in the jungle equilibrium. However, in the case of competitive equilibrium, the order is determined by the existence of a "top-trading cycle" which indicates the parties' joint interest in making an exchange, whereas in the jungle the order is determined by power, independently of the agents' preferences.

Given that the preference relations are assumed to be strict, there is a unique competitive equilibrium allocation (for a proof, see Osborne and Rubinstein (2023)). However, this allocation can be supported by many price systems, and it can even be that one house is more expensive than another in one equilibrium price system but less expensive in another.

The two fundamental welfare theorems hold for the competitive equilibrium in this model:

(a) Any competitive equilibrium $\langle (p_x),(x^i) \rangle$ is Pareto-optimal since if $(y^i) \in F$ Pareto dominates (x^i) then $p_{y^i} \geq p_{x^i}$ for all i with strict inequality for any agent i for whom $y^i \succ^i x^i$ and thus $\Sigma_{i \in N} \, p_{y^i} > \Sigma_{i \in N} \, p_{x^i}$ which contradicts the fact that the two sums must be equal.

(b) For any Pareto-optimal allocation (x^i) there is a price vector (p_x) such that $\langle (p_x),(x^i) \rangle$ is a competitive equilibrium. By Proposition 1.5 a competitive equilibrium exists for the extended economy with the initial allocation (x^i). Its allocation (y^i) is weakly Pareto superior to (x^i) and since (x^i) is Pareto-optimal it must coincide with (x^i). Therefore, if we start with $(e^i) = (x^i)$ the proof constructs a competitive equilibrium in which each agent i keeps x^i.

Power and Wealth: Since the jungle equilibrium is Pareto optimal, it can be supported by prices as a competitive equilibrium. This invites a natural question: what is the relationship between power and wealth?

First, there is always a price system in which "stronger" in the jungle economy means "richer" in the competitive equilibrium of the extended housing economy with the initial endowment profile being the jungle equilibrium of the jungle economy. Formally, let (x^i) be the jungle equilibrium in the housing economy jungle $\langle N, X, (\succsim^i)_{i \in N}, F, \rhd \rangle$. The extended housing economy $\langle N, X, (\succsim^i)_{i \in N}, F, (e^i = x^i)_{i \in N} \rangle$ has a competitive equilibrium $\langle (p_x),(x^i) \rangle$ where $p_{x^i} > p_{x^j}$ whenever $i \rhd j$. However, other equilibrium price vectors may exist. For example, if the strongest agent top-ranks his own house while all other agents bottom-rank it, then there also exists a competitive price vector in which the strongest agent is the poorest.

In fact, if we modify the economy somewhat, then there may be no jungle equilibrium in which the statement "stronger = richer" holds. For example, recall the clubs economy where each agent chooses one club from the set X, and no more than q_x agents can choose club x. Consider the economy with 4 agents, where $X = \{a, b\}$ and $q_a = q_b = 2$. If the preferences are such that agent 1 prefers a and all other agents prefer b, then the unique jungle equilibrium is (a, b, b, a). However, in this equilibrium, every agent obtains his first-best club except for agent 4 and to prevent agent 4 from getting what he wants it must be that $p_b > p_a$. Thus, any price vector which supports the jungle equilibrium allocation must have the property that the strongest agent is the poorest.

1.4   Comments on the Jungle Equilibrium

Comparative statics: The jungle equilibrium satisfies the expected comparative statics property that advancing an agent in the power ranking cannot hurt the agent. To see this, recall that there is a unique jungle equilibrium and it can be calculated via a serial dictatorship procedure. When an individual agent becomes stronger, all agents who are still stronger than him will continue to make the same choices, while the individual now gets to choose earlier and, therefore, has a strictly larger set of houses to choose from.

On the other hand, in the case of competitive equilibrium, improving an agent's initial house endowment, according to his own preferences, might make him worse off in equilibrium. Although the new house is better for him, it might be unattractive to other agents. Thus, when applying the top-trading cycle algorithm, it could be that he initially appeared in the first cycle and, after the "improvement", he now appears in the last cycle and, therefore, ends up worse off in the new equilibrium than in the old one.

Manipulability: The jungle equilibrium is immune to preference misrepresentations by an agent. Again, the unique jungle equilibrium can be calculated by the serial dictatorship algorithm. When it is an agent's turn to choose, the set of alternatives that he chooses from is unaffected by his declared preferences, and, thus, he can do no better by misrepresenting his preferences. This non-manipulability property also holds for competitive equilibria.

Indifferences: Even if some of the agents' preferences are not strict, the serial dictatorship procedure still produces a jungle equilibrium. However, it is not necessarily unique since, when an agent has to make a choice, he might have more than one maximal option and each produces a different equilibrium. Note that indifferences can also create a multiplicity of competitive equilibrium profiles in the housing economy market.

Equilibrium and Dynamics: The jungle equilibrium concept is static, like most solution concepts in Economic Theory. The following is an example of dynamics that lead to a jungle equilibrium: At the beginning, all agents are assigned to be "*homeless*". At stage $t + 1$, given the assignment of the agents at stage t to $X \cup \{homeless\}$, every homeless agent chooses his favourite house from among those that, at the end of stage t, are either: i) vacant or ii) assigned to an agent weaker than him. Every agent who currently occupies a house chooses to stay there. At the end of stage $t + 1$, if a house is chosen by only one agent, then he settles there. If more than one agent chooses the same house, then the strongest among them settles there and all the rest remain *homeless*.

Proposition 1.6: Equilibrium Dynamics

The above dynamics converges in at most n stages to the jungle equilibrium.

Proof:

Let H_t be the set of homeless agents at the beginning of stage t and i_t be the most powerful among them. If there are any homeless agents at stage $t + 1$, then $i_t \rhd i_{t+1}$: To see why, note that at stage t, i_t will obtain a home because all homeless agents are weaker than him and so he will win at any home which he approaches. Furthermore, all agents stronger than i_t remain in their homes as no one challenges them. Thus, in the beginning of stage $t + 1$, all homeless agents must be weaker than i_t. Therefore, after at most n stages, all agents have a home and the process terminates at a profile (x^i).

Suppose that (x^i) is different than the jungle equilibrium profile (y^i). Take i to be the strongest agent for whom $x^i \neq y^i$. Thus, $i \rhd j$ where j is the agent who holds y^i, i.e. $x^j = y^i$.

By Proposition 1.2, y^i is $\succ^i$-maximum in $X - \{y^1, \ldots, y^{i-1}\} = X - \{x^1, \ldots, x^{i-1}\}$ and therefore $y^i \succ^i x^i$. At the stage in the algorithm where i selected x^i it must be that y^i was being held by someone stronger than

> i. But, in the algorithm, when a house changes hands, it can only go to someone stronger so as it eventually reaches j it must be that $j \rhd i$, a contradiction.

A different power relation for each house: A key assumption in the jungle model is the uniformity of the power relation: if an agent i is able to evict agent j from one house, then he is able to evict him from any house. An extension of the model allows for dependence of the power relation on the house in dispute. Suppose that, for each house $x \in X$, there is a strict power ordering $\rhd_x$ where $i \rhd_x j$ means that agent i is stronger than agent j in a fight over house x. That is, if agent j occupies x and $i \rhd_x j$, then agent i can confiscate x if he wishes to do so. An equilibrium in the economy with house-dependent power relations $\langle N, X, (\succsim^i)_{i \in N}, F, (\rhd_x)_{x \in X} \rangle$ is a profile (x^i) such that there are no two agents i and j such that i prefers the house occupied by j to the house he occupies $(x^j \succ^i x^i)$ and i is stronger than j regarding x^j $(i \rhd_{x^j} j)$.

As commented on in Rubinstein and Yıldız (2022), the notion of a jungle equilibrium in $\langle N, X, (\succsim^i)_{i \in N}, F, (\rhd_x)_{x \in X} \rangle$ is equivalent to pairwise stability in the two-sided matching problem between N and X where each agent $i \in N$ has the preference $\succsim^i$ over X and each house $x \in X$ has the preference relation $\rhd_x$ over N. An assignment (x^i) is pairwise stable if there is no pair i and x^j such that i prefers x^j over x^i $(x^j \succ^i x^i)$ and x^j "prefers" i over j $(i \rhd_{x^j} j)$. Therefore, an assignment is pairwise stable in the auxiliary matching problem if and only if it is a jungle equilibrium with house-dependent power relations.

Gale and Shapley (1962) showed, using the deferred acceptance algorithm, that a pairwise stable matching exists in any two-sided matching problem. Thus, in the jungle with house-dependent power relations, a jungle equilibrium also exists. Since the pairwise stable matching need not be unique, neither is the jungle equilibrium when the power relation is house-dependent. Finally, Gale and Sotomayor (1985)'s analysis implies that there is always a jungle equilibrium (x^i) which is *weakly* Pareto optimal, in the sense that there is no assignment (z^i) such that $z^i \succ^i x^i$ for every $i \in N$.

1.5   The Division Jungle

We now apply the jungle concept to a version of the division economy. To the definition of a division economy from Chapter 0, we add a profile $(X^i)_{i \in N}$ of personal consumption sets, which represent bounds on each agent's ability to consume. These sets can be thought of as either physical limits on what a person can consume or what possessions he can protect. Note that, in the housing economy, there is an implicit assumption of a similar nature, namely that an agent can hold only one house. The following is the formal definition of a jungle division economy (throughout, when comparing bundles, the notation $x \le y$ means that $x_k \le y_k$ for every commodity k):

Definition: Jungle Division Economy

A **jungle division economy** is a tuple $\langle N, (X^i)_{i \in N}, (\succsim^i)_{i \in N}, F, \triangleright \rangle$ where:

- $N = \{1, \ldots, n\}$ is the set of agents.

- $X^i \subseteq \mathbb{R}_+^K$ is agent i's personal consumption set in a K-commodity world. The sets X^i are assumed to be compact, convex, and satisfy free disposal (that is, if $x^i \in X^i$, $y \in \mathbb{R}_+^K$ and $y \le x^i$, then $y \in X^i$).

- $\succsim^i$ are preferences over X^i and assumed to satisfy continuity, strict monotonicity, and strict convexity.

- F is the set of all profiles of bundles (x^i) such that:
    (i) $x^i \in X^i$ for all i, and
    (ii) $\Sigma_{i \in N} x^i \le e$ where $e \in \mathbb{R}_+^K$ is an aggregate bundle available for distribution among the agents.

- $\triangleright$ is a strict power ordering over N.

Given a profile (x^i), denote the "leftover" bundle $e - \Sigma_{i \in N} x^i$ as x^0.

We now turn to modifying the definition of a *jungle equilibrium* to fit the division jungle. There are (at least) two possible definitions that coincide with that of the housing economy. The first is a *strong jungle equilibrium* which is a feasible profile such that no agent can assemble a preferable bundle by combining his own bundle with *all* bundles held by weaker agents and the leftover bundle. By this definition, the stability of a profile is disturbed by the possibility that an agent can attack more than one weaker agent. The second definition is a *weak jungle equilibrium*, which is a feasible profile such that no agent can assemble a preferable bundle by combining his own bundle with *one* other that is either held by a weaker agent or is the leftover bundle. Formally:

Definition: Strong Jungle Equilibrium

A **strong jungle equilibrium** is a feasible profile (x^i) with the property that there is no agent i and bundle $y^i \in X^i$ such that:

(i) $y^i \succ^i x^i$.

(ii) $y^i \leq x^i + \Sigma_{i \rhd j} x^j + x^0$ (the agent takes from weaker agents and from the leftover bundle and potentially disposes of some of his possessions).

Definition: Weak Jungle Equilibrium

A **weak jungle equilibrium** is a feasible profile (x^i) with the property that there is no agent i and bundle $y^i \in X^i$ such that:

(i) $y^i \succ^i x^i$.

(ii) Either (a) or (b) holds.

    (a) $y^i \leq x^i + x^j$ for some j for whom $i \rhd j$ (the agent steals from a single weaker agent and then may dispose of some of his possessions); or

    (b) $y^i \leq x^i + x^0$ (the agent takes from the leftover bundle and then may dispose of some of his possessions).

Note that the above definitions use inequalities rather than equalities. This is because, when a stronger agent seizes other resources, he might be put outside of his consumption set and, thus, needs either to take less or to dispose of some goods in order to remain in his consumption set. Obviously, any strong jungle equilibrium is also a weak jungle equilibrium.

> ### Proposition 1.7: Strong Jungle Equilibrium: Existence and Uniqueness
>
> There exists a unique strong jungle equilibrium.

Proof:

Here again, we proceed by applying the serial dictatorship procedure and constructing a feasible profile (x^i) as follows: Start with the strongest agent 1 and define x^1 as the $\succsim^1$-best bundle in the set $\{z \in X^1 \mid z \le e\}$ which is closed and convex. Proceed inductively by defining x^i to be the $\succsim^i$-best bundle in the closed and convex set $\{z \in X^i \mid z \le e - \Sigma_{j=1}^{i-1} x^j\}$. The profile (x^i), which is feasible by construction, is a strong jungle equilibrium. By the same proof as that of Proposition 1.2, the equilibrium is unique.

Monotonicity is not used in the above proof. For existence, only continuity of the preference relations is needed to ensure that the inductive procedure used in the proof leads to a strong jungle equilibrium. Strict convexity guarantees uniqueness.

Example: The Pie Jungle

In the **pie jungle**, there is a single pie of size 1. The consumption set for every agent i is $X^i = X = [0,1]$ where $x \in X$ is interpreted as taking x of the pie. We deviate slightly from the assumptions made above and assume that every agent i has strictly convex preferences on X with a peak at $peak^i$ (and thus the preferences are not monotonic). In this case, the weak and strong jungle equilibria coincide, and the unique strong jungle equilibrium is as follows: Let m be the minimal number for which $\Sigma_{i=1,\dots,m} peak^i > 1$. Each of the $m-1$ strongest agents chooses his own peak, the mth agent gets the leftovers and the rest get nothing. If there is no such m, that is, if $\Sigma_{i=1,\dots,n} peak^i \le 1$, then all agents choose their respective peaks.

Is there a weak jungle equilibrium that is not a strong jungle equilibrium? The following proposition (whose proof is more technical than the others in the book) states that the two definitions are equivalent under "smoothness" assumptions on both the agents' preferences and on the consumption sets. Essentially, smoothness means that indifference curves and the frontiers of the consumption sets are smooth, in the sense that there is a unique tangent at any point. Formally, we will use the term *smooth* to describe an economy if the following holds for every i:

- Agent i's preference relation is represented by a strictly quasiconcave, increasing and continuously differentiable utility function $u^i : \mathbb{R}_+^K \to \mathbb{R}$, with a strictly positive gradient vector $\nabla u^i(x)$ at every bundle x.

- There exists a strictly quasiconvex and continuously differentiable function $g^i : \mathbb{R}_+^K \to \mathbb{R}$ such that $X^i = \{x^i \in \mathbb{R}_+^K \mid g^i(x^i) \leq 0\}$ with a gradient $\nabla g^i(x)$ that is a strictly positive vector at every bundle x.

Proposition 1.8: Equivalence of the Jungle Equilibrium Definitions

For a smooth jungle economy, the two definitions of jungle equilibrium coincide.

Proof:

Let (x^i) be a weak jungle equilibrium which is different than the strong jungle equilibrium (y^i). We can suppose that $x^1 \neq y^1$, since otherwise induction could be applied to the jungle economy with players $N\backslash\{1\}$ and an adjusted endowment vector $e - x^1$.

The bundle y^1 is the unique $\succ^1$-maximum bundle in $\{x \in X^1 \mid x \leq e\}$. Therefore, $y^1 \succ^1 x^1$ and in turn $e_k \geq y_k^1 > x_k^1$ for some k. Thus, $x^1 \neq e$. Also, it must be that $g^1(x^1) = 0$. If not, that is $g^1(x^1) < 0$, then since $e_k > x_k^1$, agent 1 could improve upon x^1 by seizing a small amount of good k either from an agent who holds some of that good (recall that agent 1 is the strongest agent) or from the leftovers, contradicting that (x^i) is a weak jungle equilibrium.

By definition, $u^1(y^1) > u^1(x^1)$ and $g^1(y^1) \leq g^1(x^1) = 0$. Perturb y^1 by removing a small amount of good k (for which $y_k^1 > x_k^1$) so that, by continuity, $u^1(y^1) > u^1(x^1)$ and $g^1(y^1) < g^1(x^1)$. Then, by the assumptions that u^1 is strictly quasiconcave and that $\nabla u^1(x^1) \neq 0$, it follows that $\nabla u^1(x^1) \cdot (y^1 - x^1) > 0$. Likewise, it follows that $\nabla g^1(x^1) \cdot (y^1 - x^1) < 0$. By the Lemma below, there is a vector z in $\mathbb{R}^K$ such that (i) $z_k > 0$ for some k for which $y_k^1 - x_k^1 > 0$; (ii) $z_l < 0$ for some l for which $y_l^1 - x_l^1 < 0$; (iii) $z_h = 0$ for all $h \neq k, l$; and (iv) $\nabla u^1(x^1) \cdot z > 0$ and $\nabla g^1(z^1) \cdot z < 0$. That is, z is a vector which is non-zero in only two components, k and l. With respect to k, the component z_k is positive, and the fact that $y_k^1 > x_k^1$ means there is an $i \neq 1$ (which can be 0) such that $x_k^i > 0$. With respect to l, the component z_l is negative, and the fact that $y_l^1 < x_l^1$ means that $x_l^1 > 0$. By (iv), for small enough $\varepsilon > 0$, adding εz_k units of commodity k and subtracting $-\varepsilon z_l$ units of commodity l strictly improves agent 1's utility and keeps him within his consumption set. Let ε be small enough so that εz_k units of commodity k can be taken from one weaker agent (or from the leftover x^0). This contradicts (x^i) being a weak equilibrium.

Lemma:

Let a and b be strictly positive vectors in $\mathbb{R}^n$, and suppose that $a \cdot z > 0$ and $b \cdot z < 0$ for some $z \in \mathbb{R}^n$. Then, there exists $\Delta \in \mathbb{R}^n$ such that: (i) $\Delta_k > 0$ for some k for which $z_k > 0$; (ii) $\Delta_l < 0$ for some l for which $z_l < 0$; (iii) $\Delta_h = 0$ for all $h \neq k, l$; and (iv) $a \cdot \Delta > 0$ and $b \cdot \Delta < 0$.

Proof:

First note that there are l and k such that $z_l < 0$ and $z_k > 0$. Define $\lambda_m = \frac{a_m}{b_m}$ for every m. Let λ_h be the smallest λ_l associated with $z_l < 0$. It is impossible that $\lambda_h \geq \lambda_k$ for all k such that $z_k > 0$, since in that case $a \cdot z = \sum_{i=1}^n \lambda_i z_i b_i \leq \sum_{i=1}^n \lambda_h z_i b_i = \lambda_h b \cdot z$, contradicting $b \cdot z$ being negative and $a \cdot z$ being positive. Thus, there is k such that $\lambda_h < \lambda_k$ and $z_k > 0$. Any vector $\Delta = (0, \ldots, 0, \Delta_k, 0, \ldots, 0, \Delta_h, 0, \ldots, 0)$ satisfying $\Delta_k > 0$, $\Delta_h < 0$ and $\frac{b_k}{b_h} < \frac{-\Delta_h}{\Delta_k} < \frac{a_k}{a_h}$. Thus, $a \cdot \Delta > 0$ and $b \cdot \Delta < 0$.

1.6 The Division Jungle: Comments on Welfare

The first fundamental welfare theorem: For the division economy, a first fundamental welfare theorem still holds, namely, the strong jungle equilibrium is Pareto optimal. The proof is similar to that of the housing economy: Suppose (z^i) is a strong jungle equilibrium which is not Pareto optimal. Let $(y^i) \in F$ be a Pareto-superior profile. Let j be the strongest agent for whom $y^j \neq z^j$. Both y^j and z^j belong to the set $\{x^j \in X^j \mid x^j \le e - \Sigma_{i=1}^{j-1} y^i\} = \{x^j \in X^j \mid x^j \le e - \Sigma_{i=1}^{j-1} z^i\}$. Since z^j is j's unique top-ranked bundle in this set, it holds that $z^j \succ^j y^j$, a contradiction. Note that for non-smooth economies a weak jungle equilibrium might be not Pareto optimal.

The second fundamental welfare theorem: On the other hand, the second fundamental welfare theorem cannot have an analogue for the division jungle. This is because in the division jungle there are finitely many power relations and typically infinitely many Pareto-optimal profiles. This cardinality mismatch implies that for a division economy, not every Pareto-optimal profile can be obtained as a jungle equilibrium by appending some power relation to that economy.

Power and wealth: Making a statement about the relation between power and wealth in the division economy is more involved than in the housing economy since the existence of a competitive equilibrium price vector that supports the jungle equilibrium is not guaranteed, even if all of the agents' consumption sets are the same. For a discussion of this issue, see Piccione and Rubinstein (2007).

1.7   A Didactic Perspective

The discussion in this chapter also has a didactic purpose, as expressed in the personal concluding remarks made by one of us in Piccione and Rubinstein (2007), which are essentially quoted here (with some small changes):

> When I present the model in public lectures, I ask the audience to imagine that they are attending the first lecture of a course at the University of the Jungle, entitled Introduction to the Principles of Economics. The analogy of such a presentation to the way we introduce the market equilibrium in a standard Microeconomics course serves as a device to shed light on the implicit message that Microeconomics students receive from us.
>
> Being faithful to the classical economic tradition, the jungle model does not stray far from the standard exchange economy. We use terminology that is familiar to any economics student. After having defined the notion of jungle equilibrium, we conduct the same type of analysis that can be found in any microeconomics textbook on competitive equilibrium. We show existence and then discuss the first and second fundamental welfare theorems. We emphasise the analogy between the initial endowments in an exchange economy and the initial distribution of power in the jungle: both are used to determine the equilibrium distribution of commodities among the agents. Were I teaching this model, I would also add the standard comments regarding externalities and the place for government intervention.
>
> There are arguments which attempt to dismiss the comparison between markets and jungles:
>
> One might argue that the market has the virtue of providing incentives to "produce" and to enlarge the size of the "pie" to

be distributed among the agents. On the other hand, one could also argue that the jungle provides incentives to develop power. In the market economy, agents invest effort in producing more goods. In the jungle economy, agents invest effort in becoming stronger, an asset for a society that needs to defend itself against invaders or invade others in order to accumulate resources.

One might argue that market mechanisms preserve resources that would otherwise have been wasted in conflict. Note, however, that under complete information a stronger agent can persuade a weaker one to part with his goods using only the threat of force. Societies often create rituals that help individuals gauge the power of others and thereby avoid the costs of conflict. Under incomplete information, the market also wastes resources. And finally, I have not mentioned the obvious transaction costs that are also associated with market institutions.

One might argue that labour is a good that should be treated differently. However, the long history of slavery shows this to be inaccurate.

One might also argue that the virtue of the market system is that it exploits people's natural desire to acquire wealth. In contrast, the jungle just uses people's natural willingness to exercise power and to dominate.

Obviously, I am not arguing in favour of adopting the jungle system. The comparison between the jungle and market mechanisms depends on our assessment of the characteristics with which agents enter the model. If the distribution of the initial holdings in the market reflects social values that we wish to promote, we might regard the market outcome as agreeable.

However, if the initial wealth is allocated unfairly, dishonestly or arbitrarily, then we might not favour the market system. Similarly, if power is desirable then we might advocate for the jungle system, but if the distribution of power reflects brute force that threatens lives then we would clearly not be in favour.

2 The Permissible and the Forbidden

Picture in your mind a family consisting of n members. The grandparents have prepared a holiday feast and all are sitting happily around a long table. When the main dish is served, the grandparents act as dictators, putting a portion of it on each family member's plate and making sure they eat it to the last bite. And then, dessert arrives and with it a dramatic turn of events. Grandma and Grandpa enter the room with their famous homemade pie. Everyone loves their pie and gazes eagerly at its entrance. Given the chance, each family member would gladly eat more than $1/n$ of the pie. At this point, the grandparents declare that they will not interfere in the division of the pie and will let the younger generation use their academic knowledge to decide how the pie is divided.

One member of the family, an economist, suggests that each family member should be endowed with $1/n$ of the pie and — since some perhaps appreciate the pie more, while others perhaps less — a market should operate under the table where members can exchange slices of the pie for money. Another member of the family, a game theorist, suggests that the grandparents conduct an auction. He claims that this might be fun and, more importantly, the pie will be divided optimally. Hopefully, in your family, neither markets nor auctions are used to resolve such a conflict and, instead, harmony is achieved by means of a social norm: each family member does not dare to even consider taking more than the socially acceptable amount, say q, of the pie.

Obviously, not every q will bring harmony to the family. If $q > 1/n$, then a family crisis would erupt since there would not be enough pie to satisfy the family members. All family members would race to get their slice, and some will be disappointed because they are unable to realize their anticipation of eating q of the pie. If $q < 1/n$, then no conflict arises, but the members of the family would feel uneasy looking at the leftovers on the table and, next year,

 https://doi.org/10.11647/OBP.0404.02

would feel justified in taking a bit more. If $q = 1/n$, then harmony prevails. It is optimal for each family member to take q, and any loosening of the norm will lead to demands which cannot be satisfied.

We think of a bound on the portion that one can take as an example of a natural social norm that specifies what is considered permissible ("done") and forbidden ("not done"). Such a norm resolves the family's allocation problem but not with prices or games.

Following Richter and Rubinstein (2020), we analyze the Y-equilibrium concept. It is defined as a set of permissible alternatives (which is the same for all agents) combined with a profile of choices (one for each agent) such that:

(i) each agent's choice is optimal from among the permissible alternatives;
(ii) the profile of choices is feasible; and
(iii) the set of permissible alternatives is maximal in the sense that there is no superset of permissible alternatives from which a profile satisfying (i) and (ii) can be found.

By this definition, two forces make a permissible set unstable: the first modifies the permissible set in the case that the profile of (intended) choices is not feasible, while the second loosens restrictions on the permissible set as long as a new profile of optimal choices is feasible.

The Y-equilibrium concept reflects a decentralized institution for achieving harmony in a society. We envision that, without a central authority, the same invisible hand that calculates equilibrium prices so "effectively" is also able to determine a maximal set of permissible alternatives that are compatible with self-maximizing behavior. The above forces adjust the social norm until harmony is achieved. While we do not provide a general dynamic process that converges to Y-equilibrium, in Richter and Rubinstein (2020), for several examples, we demonstrated natural *tâtonnement*-like processes that lead to a Y-equilibrium.

We now proceed to the formal definition of the equilibrium notion.

2.1   The Y-Equilibrium Concept

Recall that an *economy* is a tuple $\langle N, X, (\succsim^i)_{i \in N}, F \rangle$ where N is the set of agents, X is the set of alternatives that each agent chooses from, $\succsim^i$ is agent i's preferences on X, and $F \subseteq X^N$ is the set of feasible choice profiles.

A candidate for an equilibrium is a *configuration* which consists of a subset of X, called a permissible set, together with a profile of choices:

> **Definition: Configuration**
>
> A **configuration** is a pair $\langle Y, (y^i)_{i \in N} \rangle$ where $Y \subseteq X$ and $(y^i)_{i \in N}$ is a profile of elements in Y. We refer to Y as a **permissible set** and to $(y^i)_{i \in N}$ as an **outcome**.

As explained in Chapter 0, a candidate for a solution in this book has a structure analogous to that of a competitive equilibrium. It is comprised of a profile of choices (one for each agent) and an additional parameter. In a configuration, the additional parameter is a permissible set, that is taken by all agents as given and uniformly binds the choices of all agents. Analogously, in a competitive equilibrium, the additional parameter is a price system, that is taken by all agents as given and uniformly binds the exchanges of all agents.

Before defining the equilibrium concept, we need an additional concept: a para-equilibrium is a configuration where each individual maximizes his interests given the permissible set and the resulting choice profile is feasible.

> **Definition: Para-equilibrium**
>
> A **para-equilibrium** is a configuration $\langle Y, (y^i) \rangle$ satisfying:
> (i) For all i, y^i is a $\succsim^i$-maximal alternative in Y.
> (ii) The profile (y^i) is in F.

A Y-equilibrium is a para-equilibrium such that any expansion of the permissible set will lead to a violation of feasibility if agents self-maximize with respect to the expanded permissible set.

Definition: Y-equilibrium

A **Y-equilibrium** is a para-equilibrium $\langle Y, (y^i) \rangle$ such that there is no para-equilibrium $\langle Z, (z^i) \rangle$ for which Z is a strict superset of Y.

As mentioned earlier, we view the permissible set not as being determined by an authority but, rather, as evolving through an invisible-hand-like process with two forces: First, if the profile of intended choices from the permissible set is not feasible, then alternatives are removed or added to the permissible set. Second, when the profile of chosen alternatives is feasible, additional alternatives are added to the permissible set as long as harmony is not disturbed. Note that (y^i) can differ from (z^i), that is, when assessing the existence of a larger permissible set, choices can adapt to the loosening.

We take the permissible set to be uniform for all agents, although we are aware that there are situations in life where norms are nonuniform, such as allowing handicapped drivers to park in places where others are not permitted. The uniformity of the permissible set in our model is analogous to the uniformity of the price system in models of competitive equilibrium (although prices are often not uniform in real life). In some circumstances, uniformity can be viewed as an expression of equality of opportunity. It also is a simplicity property: in order to be followed, norms must be simple and clear, and norms are simpler when they do not distinguish between agents based on their names or preferences.

Example: A Housing Economy

Consider the housing economy with $N = \{1, 2\}$, $X = \{a, b, c, d, e\}$, and preferences $a \succ^1 b \succ^1 c \succ^1 d \succ^1 e$ and $a \succ^2 c \succ^2 b \succ^2 e \succ^2 d$. One para-equilibrium is $Y = \{d, e\}$, $y^1 = d$, $y^2 = e$. This is not a Y-equilibrium since $Y = \{b, c, d, e\}$ with $y^1 = b$, $y^2 = c$ is also a para-equilibrium with a larger permissible set. The latter is the unique Y-equilibrium since the alternative a cannot be a member of any para-equilibrium permissible set as it is the top-ranked for both agents. Incidentally, the Y-equilibrium outcome is not Pareto-optimal because a is left unassigned.

Existence: Not every economy has a Y-equilibrium. In any housing economy, if at least two agents have the same strict preferences over the houses, then no Y-equilibrium exists. This is because, whatever the permissible set is, those two agents will pick the same house, which violates feasibility. This demonstrates that social norms regarding "the permissible and the forbidden" do not resolve conflicts when agents have similar preferences yet feasibility requires them to make different choices.

Example: A Single Pie

Consider the grandparents' pie economy discussed in the beginning of the chapter. There are n family members, and a pie of size 1 is to be divided among them. The set of alternatives is $X = [0, 1]$ where $x \in X$ is a share of the pie. Each agent prefers to get as large a share as possible. The feasibility constraint states that the sum of their choices cannot exceed 1 (though some pie can be left over).

To see that this economy has a unique Y-equilibrium, notice first that the pair $\langle Y = [0, 1/n], (y^i \equiv 1/n) \rangle$ is a para-equilibrium. There is no para-equilibrium with a point above $1/n$ in the permissible set since, then, every agent would choose a point above $1/n$, which is not feasible. Therefore, the above pair is a Y-equilibrium. There is no other Y-equilibrium since the permissible set in any para-equilibrium is a subset of $[0, 1/n]$.

Example: The Quorum Economy

Consider an economy with a finite set of clubs, X. Agents have preferences over the clubs (without regard to the clubs' memberships). In order to operate, each club x needs a minimal quorum of $m_x \leq n$

(rather than having a maximal capacity as in the clubs economy). That is, feasibility requires that each club x is either empty or chosen by at least m_x members. A special case is the consensus economy where $m_x = n$ for all x, that is, feasibility requires that all agents make the same choice.

In general, if every agent were to choose his favourite club, then there would be non-empty clubs with less than a quorum. The role of the permissible set is to help the agents to coordinate their choices while imposing minimal restrictions on the permissible clubs.

A Y-equilibrium always exists: First, a para-equilibrium exists because any configuration $Y = \{x\}$ combined with all agents choosing x is a para-equilibrium. Second, since the set of subsets of X is finite, there is a para-equilibrium with a permissible set that cannot be expanded.

However, Pareto optimality is not guaranteed, as illustrated by the following example. Let $n = 6$, $X = \{a, b, c\}$, and $m_x = 3$ for all x. Two agents have the preferences $a \succ b \succ c$, two have the preferences $b \succ c \succ a$, and two have the preferences $c \succ a \succ b$. Obviously, there is no para-equilibrium with $Y = X$. Furthermore, there is no para-equilibrium with exactly two permissible clubs since four of the agents would choose one club and only two would choose the other, violating feasibility. As above, having a single club open is a para-equilibrium and since there are no multi-club para-equilibria, it is a Y-equilibrium. Thus, there are three Y-equilibria, each with a single different club open. Each Y-equilibrium outcome is not Pareto-optimal since there is an unopened club that is strictly preferred by four agents and, therefore, there is a Pareto improvement where exactly three of those four agents switch to that more-preferred club.

The Y-equilibrium concept is not meant to be normative in any sense. However, it has two fairness properties:

(i) All agents face the same choice set. Analogously, in the standard competitive equilibrium, all agents face the same trading opportunities.

(ii) It is envy-free (see Foley (1966) and Varian (1974)). Envy-freeness ensures that no agent can complain that someone else is assigned an alternative that he prefers.

> **Definition: Envy-freeness**
>
> A profile $(y^i)_{i \in N}$ is **envy-free** if, for all $i \neq j$, $y^i \succsim^i y^j$.

The concepts of para-equilibrium and envy-freeness are closely related. A profile is envy-free if and only if it is the outcome of some para-equilibrium: First, any para-equilibrium outcome is envy-free (no agent can envy another's choice since all agents choose from the same set). Second, if a profile (y^i) is envy-free, then $\langle \{y^1, \ldots, y^n\}, (y^i) \rangle$ is a para-equilibrium.

2.2 Y-Equilibrium, Pareto Optimality, and Envy-Freeness

We have seen that Y-equilibrium profiles need not be overall Pareto-optimal. Nonetheless, they still satisfy some efficiency criterion. We now show that the Y-equilibrium profiles are precisely those which are Pareto optimal *from among the set of feasible envy-free profiles*.

> **Proposition 2.1: Y-equilibrium Outcome Characterization**
>
> A profile is a Y-equilibrium outcome if and only if it is Pareto-optimal among all feasible envy-free profiles.

> **Proof:**
>
> Let $\langle Y, (y^i) \rangle$ be a Y-equilibrium. The profile (y^i) is feasible and envy-free. If it is not Pareto-optimal among the feasible envy-free profiles, then there is a feasible envy-free profile (z^i) that Pareto-dominates (y^i). The configuration $\langle Y \cup \{z^1, \ldots, z^n\}, (z^i) \rangle$ is a para-equilibrium (since $z^i \succsim^i z^j$ for all i, j, and $z^i \succsim^i y^i \succsim^i y$ for all i and $y \in Y$). By Pareto dominance, $z^i \succ^i y^i$ for at least one agent i and therefore $z^i \notin Y$. Thus, $Y \cup \{z^1, \ldots, z^n\}$ is a strict superset of Y, contradicting the definition of Y-equilibrium.

In the other direction, let (y^i) be Pareto-optimal among the feasible envy-free profiles. Let Y be the set of all elements in this profile plus any element which is weakly inferior to y^i for every agent i, namely, $Y = \bigcup_i \{y^i\} \cup \{x \mid \text{for all } i, \ y^i \succsim^i x\}$. The configuration $\langle Y, (y^i) \rangle$ is a para-equilibrium. In order to show that it is also a Y-equilibrium, we need to invalidate the existence of a para-equilibrium $\langle Z, (z^i) \rangle$ for which $Z \supsetneq Y$. If it exists, then, $z^i \succsim^i y^i$ for all i and (z^i) is envy-free. Let $x \in Z - Y$. By the definition of Y, there is an agent j for whom $x \succ^j y^j$ and, consequently, $z^j \succsim^j x \succ^j y^j$. Therefore, (z^i) is a feasible envy-free profile that Pareto-dominates (y^i), contradicting (y^i) being Pareto-optimal among the feasible envy-free profiles. Thus, no such para-equilibrium $\langle Z, (z^i) \rangle$ exists and, therefore, $\langle Y, (y^i) \rangle$ is a Y-equilibrium.

We do not take overall Pareto optimality as a necessary condition for the plausibility or desirability of a solution concept. Still, a natural question is: What condition guarantees that any Y-equilibrium outcome is overall Pareto-optimal (and not just among the envy-free profiles)? One such condition is the *imitation property*: F satisfies the imitation property if, whenever a profile is in F, so is any profile for which one agent adopts the alternative chosen by another agent instead of his own. That is, for any $(a^i) \in F$ and any $i, j \in N$, the profile where a^i is replaced with a^j is also in F. An example where the imitation property holds is the stay close economy (described in Chapter 0) since, if one agent adopts another's position, the maximal distance between any two agents does not increase.

Proposition 2.2: The Imitation Property and Pareto Optimality

Assume that F satisfies the imitation property. Then, a profile is a Y-equilibrium outcome if and only if it is overall Pareto optimal.

> **Proof:**
>
> Let $\langle Y, (y^i) \rangle$ be a Y-equilibrium. Assume by contradiction that there is a feasible profile (z^i) which Pareto-dominates (y^i). We construct a profile (x^i) as follows: Assign x^1, a $\succsim^1$-maximal alternative from $\{z^1, ..., z^N\}$, to agent 1. Assign x^2, a $\succsim^2$-maximal alternative from $\{x^1, z^2, ..., z^N\}$, to agent 2, and so on. In this construction, the profile selected at each stage is feasible (due to the imitation property) and $x^i \succsim^i z^i$ for all i. Furthermore, for every agent i, the alternative x^i is $\succsim^i$-maximal from $\{x^1, ..., x^{i-1}, z^i, ..., z^N\} \supseteq \{x^1, ..., x^N\}$. Thus, (x^i) is feasible and envy-free. It weakly Pareto-dominates (z^i) and thus Pareto-dominates (y^i), contradicting Proposition 2.1.
>
> The other direction follows immediately from Proposition 2.1 because, under the imitation condition on F, every Pareto-optimal profile is envy-free and, therefore, is also Pareto-optimal among the envy-free allocations.

2.3 Euclidean Economies

In many common economic models, such as Walrasian economies, the set of alternatives is taken to be a subset of a Euclidean space with standard closedness, convexity, and differentiability restrictions on the alternatives, the preference relations, and the feasibility set. We now consider our framework in a Euclidean setting.

> **Definition: Euclidean Economy**
>
> A **Euclidean economy** is an economy $\langle N, X, (\succsim^i)_{i \in N}, F \rangle$ such that:
> (i) The set X is a closed subset of some Euclidean space.
> (ii) For each i, the preferences $\succsim^i$ are continuous.
> (iii) The feasibility set F is anonymous (closed under permutations), compact, and contains at least one constant profile.

A Euclidean economy is **convex** if X, F, and the preferences are convex.

A Euclidean economy is **differentiable** if the preferences are strictly convex and differentiable (i.e. have differentiable utility representations or, more generally, satisfy the condition suggested in Rubinstein (2005)).

Note that in any Y-equilibrium of a Euclidean economy, the permissible set must be closed since, if $\langle Y, (y^i) \rangle$ is a para-equilibrium, then by continuity, $\langle cl(Y), (y^i) \rangle$ is also a para-equilibrium. We now show that any Euclidean economy has a Y-equilibrium.

Proposition 2.3: Existence of a Y-equilibrium in Euclidean Economies

Every Euclidean economy has a Y-equilibrium.

Proof:

Let *EFF* be the set of envy-free feasible profiles. It is non-empty because there is a feasible constant profile (which is trivially envy-free). It is closed since F is closed, and envy-freeness is defined by weak inequalities and preferences are continuous. It is compact because it is a closed subset of F, which is a compact set.

Since each $\succsim^i$ is continuous and X is a subset of a Euclidean space, there is a continuous utility function u^i representing $\succsim^i$. Thus, there is at least one profile $(z^i) \in EFF$ that maximizes $\Sigma_i u^i(x^i)$ over *EFF* and, therefore, it is Pareto optimal in *EFF*. By Proposition 2.1, (z^i) is a Y-equilibrium outcome.

2.4   The "Kosher" Economy

Previously, we discussed an economy in which one pie is allocated among a group of family members. We now consider an economy with two pies where each agent can consume a portion from *only one of the two pies*. We call it the

"Kosher" economy because it reminds us of the Jewish kosher rule stipulating that diners can consume either a meat dish or a dairy dish but not both. Of course, the situation where consumption is mutually exclusive is much broader and includes, for example, a situation where the two pies stand for consumption goods in two different locations at the same time (see Malinvaud (1972)). Formally, there are two pies in the economy and at least two agents. Each agent chooses a share of a single pie, that is, X consists of all objects of the type $(a, 0)$, which represents consuming a share $a \in [0, 1]$ from the first pie and of the type $(0, b)$, which represents consuming a share $b \in [0, 1]$ from the second pie. A bundle, which consists of a strictly positive share of each pie, is not an alternative. A profile is feasible if the sum of the agents' shares of each pie does not exceed 1. Agents have continuous and strictly monotonic preferences over X.

The Kosher economy is Euclidean and thus, by Proposition 2.3, has a Y-equilibrium. We will show that its permissible set is unique and specifies a maximal quota for each pie. Furthermore, every Y-equilibrium outcome is either Pareto optimal or "almost Pareto optimal": either both pies are fully consumed and the equilibrium outcome is Pareto optimal, or one pie is fully consumed and a small amount of the other pie is wasted.

> **Claim: Y-equilibrium in the Kosher Economy**
>
> In any Kosher economy:
> (i) There is a unique Y-equilibrium permissible set.
> (ii) In any Y-equilibrium, at least one of the pies is fully consumed.
> (iii) In any Y-equilibrium, if one pie is not fully consumed, then the unallocated portion is not larger than the quota for that pie.

> **Proof:**
>
> By Proposition 2.3, a Y-equilibrium exists. As mentioned earlier, its permissible set must be closed. It also must include all dominated consumption bundles (otherwise such alternatives could be added

in without altering the agents' choices because all preferences are monotonic). Therefore, any Y-equilibrium permissible set is specified by two quotas, a_Y and b_Y, and will be denoted by $a_Y \boxplus b_Y = \{(a,0) \mid a \leq a_Y\} \cup \{(0,b) \mid b \leq b_Y\}$.

(i) Assume not. Let $\langle a_Y \boxplus b_Y, (y^i) \rangle$ and $\langle a_Z \boxplus b_Z, (z^i) \rangle$ be two Y-equilibria with different permissible sets. The permissible sets cannot be nested. Therefore, without loss of generality, it holds that $a_Y > a_Z$ and $b_Z > b_Y$. Take the permissible set $a_Y \boxplus b_Z$ and attach to each agent an optimal bundle from $\{(a_Y,0),(0,b_Z)\}$. The number of agents assigned $(a_Y,0)$ is weakly less than the number of agents assigned $(a_Y,0)$ from $a_Y \boxplus b_Y$ because any agent i for whom $(a_Y,0) \succsim^i (0,b_Z)$, also satisfies $(a_Y,0) \succ^i (0,b_Y)$. Thus, the first pie is not over-demanded. Likewise, the second pie is also not over-demanded, and thus, there is a para-equilibrium with the permissible set $a_Y \boxplus b_Z$. This set is a strict superset of the initial two permissible sets, contradicting their being Y-equilibria.

(ii) Assume not, that is, there is a Y-equilibrium $\langle a \boxplus b, (y^i) \rangle$ where k agents choose $(a,0)$ while the other $n-k$ agents choose $(0,b)$ and no pie is fully consumed, that is, $ka < 1$ and $(n-k)b < 1$.

It cannot be that $k = 0$ (or $n-k = 0$), since then $\langle a \boxplus 1/n, y^i = (0,1/n) \rangle$ is a para-equilibrium with a larger permissible set. Thus, both k and $n-k$ are positive. Let $a' = 1/k > a$ and $b' = 1/(n-k) > b$. Consider the agents' preferences over the set $a' \boxplus b'$. If at least k agents weakly prefer $(a',0)$ to $(0,b')$ and at least $n-k$ agents weakly prefer the reverse, then set $Y' = a' \boxplus b'$.

If not, then without loss of generality, suppose that strictly fewer than k agents weakly prefer $(a',0)$ to $(0,b')$. Let $b_\lambda = (1-\lambda)b + \lambda b'$. At least k agents strictly prefer $(a',0)$ to $(0,b)$. Take the maximal λ for which there are at least k agents who weakly prefer $(a',0)$ to $(0,b_\lambda)$, which exists because preferences are monotonic and continuous. At any $\gamma > \lambda$, fewer than k agents prefer $(a',0)$, so more than $n-k$ agents strictly prefer $(0,b_\gamma)$ to $(a',0)$, and therefore by continuity more than $n-k$ agents weakly prefer $(0,b_\lambda)$ to $(a',0)$. Set $Y' = a' \boxplus b_\lambda$.

In both cases, $Y' \supsetneq a \boxplus b$. In order to reach a contradiction we construct a para-equilibrium with permissible set being Y'. Let $N_a = \{i \mid (a',0) \succ^i (0,b_\lambda)\}$, $N_b = \{i \mid (0,b_\lambda) \succ^i (a',0)\}$ and $N_I = \{i \mid (a',0) \sim^i (0,b_\lambda)\}$. Since $|N_a|+|N_I| \geq k$, it follows that $|N_b| \leq n-k$. Likewise $|N_a| \leq k$. Thus, there is a para-equilibrium with permissible set Y' where all agents from N_a are assigned to pie A, all agents from N_b are assigned to pie B, and the agents in N_I are partitioned so that exactly k agents are assigned to A.

(iii) Suppose $\langle a \boxplus b, (y^i) \rangle$ is a Y-equilibrium where k agents choose $(a,0)$ and the leftover portion $1 - ka > a$. If every agent who chooses $(0,b)$ strictly prefers $(0,b)$ to $(a,0)$, then a can be slightly increased without changing consumption patterns, thus violating the maximality of the Y-equilibrium. Otherwise, there is an agent i for whom $y^i = (0,b) \sim^i (a,0)$. Then, modifying the equilibrium by assigning agent i to $(a,0)$ instead of $(0,b)$ is also a Y-equilibrium (it is a para-equilibrium and since we started with a Y-equilibrium there is no larger para-equilibrium) in which neither pie is fully consumed, contradicting (ii).

2.5   Convex Y-Equilibrium

Up until now, we have not imposed any restrictions on the structure of the permissible set. In the rest of the chapter, we will study convex Euclidean economies (which have convexity and continuity-type requirements on the set of alternatives, the preferences, and the feasible set), and we will require that the permissible set be convex.

There are two motivations for requiring a permissible set to be convex:

(i) Suppose that on a certain highway, you are told that it is permitted to drive at 20 mph and at 80 mph. Naturally, you conclude that it is also permitted to drive at 50 mph. In contrast, if you are told that it is forbidden to drive on that highway both at 20 mph and at 80 mph, you wouldn't instinctively conclude that 50 mph is also forbidden. This highlights an asymmetry between the permissible and the forbidden. Forbidden actions are usually "extreme", while permissible actions are generally a sort of "middle ground". (As always, exceptions exist: on an ice road in Estonia, it is only permitted to drive at speeds in the intervals 10–25 kph and 40–70 kph.)

(ii) As mentioned earlier, for a norm to be accepted and internalized, simplicity is a virtue. In this vein, the restriction of attention to convex permissible sets can also be viewed as a simplicity requirement. In the one-dimensional case described above, a convex permissible set is simply a minimum and maximum speed. We will demonstrate later that, in higher-dimensional spaces, the equilibrium convex permissible sets are simple in the sense that they can be described by a small number of linear inequalities.

The requirement that the permissible set is convex is similar in spirit to the standard assumption that agents choose from budget sets that are determined by common linear prices. The linearity of prices is a form of simplicity and is an attractive assumption even if in reality prices are often not linear.

Definition: Convex Y-equilibrium

A para-equilibrium $\langle Y, (y^i) \rangle$ of a convex Euclidean economy is **convex** if Y is convex. A **convex Y-equilibrium** is a convex para-equilibrium $\langle Y, (y^i) \rangle$ such that there is no other convex para-equilibrium $\langle Z, (z^i) \rangle$ with a larger permissible set $Z \supsetneq Y$.

As in the Y-equilibrium case for Euclidean economies, any convex Y-equilibrium has a closed permissible set. If not, then the closure of its permissible set, which is also convex, together with the same profile of alternatives, would constitute a convex para-equilibrium with a larger permissible set.

A Y-equilibrium with a convex permissible set is a convex Y-equilibrium. However, a convex Y-equilibrium need not be a Y-equilibrium (it might be that there is no larger convex para-equilibrium permissible set, but there is a larger non-convex para-equilibrium permissible set).

2.6 Pareto Optimality and Existence of Convex Y-Equilibrium

Proposition 2.1 states that the Y-equilibrium profiles are exactly those which are Pareto-optimal among the para-equilibrium profiles (which are the feasible envy-free profiles). For convex Y-equilibria, there is a partial analogue: profiles which are Pareto-optimal among the convex para-equilibrium profiles are convex Y-equilibria profiles. However, when discussing the exchange economy, we will see that there can be convex Y-equilibrium profiles that are not Pareto-optimal among the convex para-equilibrium profiles.

> **Proposition 2.4: A Sufficient Condition for a Profile to be a Convex Y-equilibrium Outcome**
>
> For convex Euclidean economies, any profile which is Pareto-optimal among the convex para-equilibrium outcomes is a convex Y-equilibrium outcome.

> **Proof:**
>
> Given a convex Euclidean economy, let (y^i) be a convex para-equilibrium outcome that is Pareto-optimal among the convex para-equilibrium outcomes. Let P be the collection of all convex sets Y for which $\langle Y, (y^i) \rangle$ is a convex para-equilibrium. Endow P with the partial order $\supseteq$. We will use Zorn's Lemma to show that P has a maximal element. (A reminder of Zorn's Lemma: Given a partially ordered set P, if every chain — a completely ordered subset of P — has an upper bound in P, then the set P has at least one maximal element.)

Given a chain $\mathscr{C}$ of elements in P, let U be the union of the sets in $\mathscr{C}$. Clearly, U is an upper bound on $\mathscr{C}$, and we now show that U is in P. The set U is convex since for any two points $x, y \in U$, there is some $Y \in \mathscr{C}$ such that $x, y \in Y$ and, since any convex combination of x and y is in Y, it is also in U. To show that the tuple $\langle U, (y^i) \rangle$ is a para-equilibrium, it suffices to show that, for each i, the element y^i is $\succsim^i$-maximal in U. If there is an $x \in U$ such that $x \succ^i y^i$ for some i, then there is $Y \in \mathscr{C}$ such that $x \in Y$, contradicting that $\langle Y, (y^i) \rangle$ is a para-equilibrium.

Let Y^* be a maximal element of P. It is left to show that $\langle Y^*, (y^i) \rangle$ is a Y-equilibrium. Suppose that there is a convex para-equilibrium $\langle Z, (z^i) \rangle$ such that $Z \supsetneq Y^*$. It must be that $z^i \succsim^i y^i$ for all i. Since (y^i) is Pareto-optimal from among the convex para-equilibrium outcomes, it must be that $z^i \sim^i y^i$ for all i. Then, $\langle Z, (y^i) \rangle$ is also a convex para-equilibrium, contradicting the maximality of Y^*.

For Euclidean economies, we have already shown that a Y-equilibrium always exists (Proposition 2.3). The following proposition demonstrates that a convex Y-equilibrium also exists.

Proposition 2.5: Existence of a Convex Y-equilibrium

Every convex Euclidean economy has a convex Y-equilibrium.

Proof:

Let O be the set of convex para-equilibrium outcomes. The set O is not empty since F contains a constant profile $(y^i \equiv y^*)$ and the pair $\langle \{y^*\}, (y^i \equiv y^*) \rangle$ is trivially a convex para-equilibrium.

The set O is compact. To see this, since $O \subseteq F$ and F is compact, it suffices to show that O is closed. Take a sequence $\langle Y_t, (y_t^i) \rangle$ of para-equilibria such that (y_t^i) converges to (z^i) as $t \to \infty$. Let $Z \subseteq X$ be the convex hull of the limit allocations $\{z^1, \ldots, z^n\}$. The configuration $\langle Z, (z^i) \rangle$ is a convex para-equilibrium since if there is an agent j and a convex combination of the $\{z^1, \ldots, z^n\}$ such that $\Sigma_{i \in N} \lambda^i z^i \succ^j z^j$, then by continuity, for some large enough t, $\Sigma_{i \in N} \lambda^i y_t^i \succ^j y_t^j$. Since Y_t is convex, it holds that $\Sigma_{i \in N} \lambda^i y_t^i \in Y_t$, but this violates $\langle Y_t, (y_t^i) \rangle$ being a convex para-equilibrium.

Since O is compact, the same argument as in Proposition 2.3 implies the existence of a profile that is Pareto-optimal in O and, by Proposition 2.4, it is a convex Y-equilibrium outcome.

2.7   A Structure Theorem for Convex Y-equilibrium

Much of Economic Theory deals with establishing conditions that guarantee the existence of a solution concept. Theorems about the structure of equilibrium are less common, although, in our opinion, are more interesting. We now show that our assumptions on the economy, together with a differentiability condition, guarantee that the permissible set of convex equilibria is an intersection of at most n half-spaces (recall that n is the number of agents). Thus, the requirement that the permissible set is convex implies that the convex Y-equilibrium permissible set takes a relatively simple form.

Proposition 2.6: The Structure of Convex Y-equilibria

Let $\langle Y, (y^i) \rangle$ be a convex Y-equilibrium in a differentiable Euclidean economy. Let $J = \{i \mid y^i$ is not the $\succsim^i$-global maximum in $X\}$. Then, there is a profile of closed half-spaces $(H^j)_{j \in J}$, such that $Y = \cap_{j \in J} H^j$.

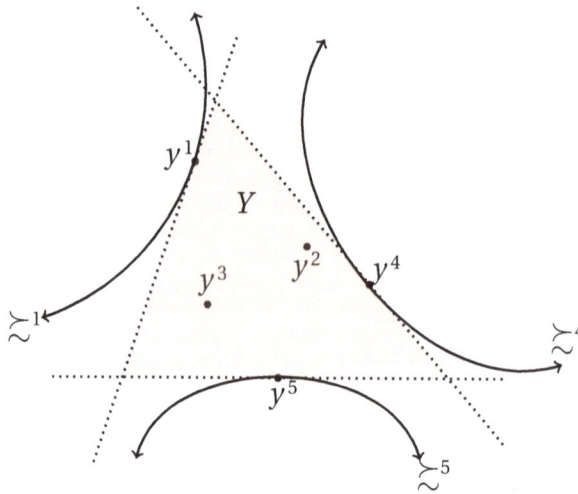

Figure 2.1 An illustration of Proposition 2.6 (note that $J = \{1, 4, 5\}$)

Proof:

First, note that if $J = \emptyset$, that is, every agent is assigned his first-best, then $Y = X$ (which is the degenerate case where Y is the intersection of an empty set of half-spaces). Otherwise, for every $j \in J$, let H^j be the unique half-space of alternatives containing y^j such that y^j is strictly preferred to all other elements in H^j. Its existence is guaranteed by the assumptions of differentiability and strict convexity of the agents' preference relations.

We first show that Y is a subset of $\cap_{j \in J} H^j$: Suppose that for some $j \in J$ there is an alternative $w^j \in Y - H^j$. By the differentiability and strict convexity of j's preferences, and for small $\varepsilon > 0$, it holds that $\varepsilon w^j + (1 - \varepsilon) y^j \succ^j y^j$. By convexity of Y it holds that $\varepsilon w^j + (1 - \varepsilon) y^j \in Y$. Therefore, y^j is not $\succsim^j$-maximal in Y, a contradiction.

To show that the permissible set Y is equal to $\cap_{j \in J} H^j$, it remains to be shown that $\langle \cap_{j \in J} H^j, (y^i) \rangle$ is a convex para-equilibrium. This follows from:

(i) The set $\cap_{j \in J} H^j$ is convex.

(ii) For each agent i, $y^i \in Y \subseteq \cap_{j \in J} H^j$.

(iii) For each $j \in J$, y^j is the $\succsim^j$-maximum in H^j and, thus, also in $\cap_{j \in J} H^j$.

(iv) For each $i \notin J$, y^i is the $\succsim^i$-global maximum and, thus, also in $\cap_{j \in J} H^j$.

2.8 The Division Economy

A leading economic problem is the division of a bundle among the members of a society. The grandparents single pie economy is its simplest version. The only convex Y-equilibrium is the intuitively appealing norm that forbids taking more than $1/n^{\text{th}}$ of the pie. For the multi-good division economy, the analogous norm which allows an agent to take up to $1/n^{\text{th}}$ of the total bundle is typically not a Y-equilibrium permissible set because it does not allow any trades. We proceed by exploring the properties of convex Y-equilibria in a differentiable division economy, formally defined as:

Definition: Differentiable Division Economy

A **differentiable division economy** $\langle N, X, (\succsim^i)_{i \in N}, F \rangle$ is a differentiable Euclidean economy such that:

(i) The set of alternatives is all bundles with m commodities, i.e. $X = \mathbb{R}^m_+$.

(ii) Every preference relation $\succsim^i$ is strictly monotonic (besides being continuous, strictly convex, and differentiable).

(iii) There is a bundle $e \in \mathbb{R}^m_{++}$ such that $(x^i) \in F$ if and only if $\Sigma_i x^i \leq e$.

The following claim draws a connection between convex Y-equilibrium and *egalitarian competitive equilibrium* (see Foley (1966) and Varian (1974)) which is a competitive equilibrium of the exchange economy in which each agent is initially endowed with $1/n$ of the total bundle. We will see that every egalitarian competitive equilibrium outcome is a convex Y-equilibrium outcome and, if at least one agent selects an interior bundle, then its permissible set is identical to the egalitarian competitive equilibrium's common budget set.

Claim: Egalitarian Competitive Equilibria and Convex Y-equilibria

Let $\langle p,(y^i)\rangle$ be an egalitarian competitive equilibrium in a differentiable division economy. Then, there is a convex Y-equilibrium with the same allocation $\langle Y,(y^i)\rangle$. Furthermore, if at least one of the bundles y^j is strictly positive, then Y must be $B = \{y \mid p \cdot y \leq p \cdot e/n\}$.

Proof:

The pair $\langle B,(y^i)\rangle$ is a convex para-equilibrium and (y^i) is overall Pareto-optimal by the standard first welfare theorem. Thus, by Proposition 2.4, (y^i) is a convex Y-equilibrium outcome.

If $\langle Y,(y^i)\rangle$ is a convex Y-equilibrium, then by Proposition 2.6, $Y = \cap_{i \in N} H^i$, where H^i is the lower half-space of $\succsim^i$ at y^i (since no agent has his first-best, it holds that $J = N$). For all i, $B \subseteq H^i$, since otherwise there exists $z^i \in B \backslash H^i$ and, by differentiability and strict convexity, y^i would not be $\succsim^i$-optimal in B. If for some j the bundle y^j has a zero coordinate, then it can be that $B \subsetneq H^j$, but if for any j the bundle y^j is strictly positive, then $H^j = B$ and, therefore, $Y = \cap_i H^i = B$.

Comments:

Every overall Pareto-optimal interior convex Y-equilibrium profile is an egalitarian competitive equilibrium allocation:

Let $\langle Y,(y^i)\rangle$ be a convex Y-equilibrium such that each bundle y^i is interior. By monotonicity, the alternative y^i is never $\succsim^i$-globally maximal and thus, by Proposition 2.6, $Y = \cap_{i \in N} H^i$ where H^i is the lower half-space of $\succsim^i$ at y^i and, by monotonicity, there is a positive vector p^i and a positive number w^i such that $H^i = \{x \mid p^i \cdot x \leq w^i\}$. Since every y^i is interior and the allocation is Pareto optimal, the half-spaces must be parallel (otherwise, any two agents on non-parallel half-spaces could make a Pareto-improving local exchange) that is, there is a positive vector p such that $p^i = p$ for all i. It follows that $Y = \{x \mid p \cdot x \leq w\}$ for some positive vector p and a positive number w. By monotonicity, $p \cdot y^i = w$ for all i. Since $p \cdot e = p \cdot \Sigma_{i \in N} y^i = nw$, we have $p \cdot y^i = w = p \cdot (e/n)$. Thus, (y^i) is a competitive egalitarian equilibrium allocation with price vector p.

There can exist a non-interior Pareto-optimal convex equilibrium outcome that is not an egalitarian competitive equilibrium allocation:

Here is a simple example: Let $n = 3$, $m = 2$, $e = (5,5)$ and the agents' preferences be represented by the utility functions specified in Figure 2.2, panel (a) (a slight modification of the preferences will make the preference relations strictly convex):

$$u^1(x_1, x_2) = x_1$$

$$u^2(x_1, x_2) = x_1 + x_2$$

$$u^3(x_1, x_2) = x_2$$

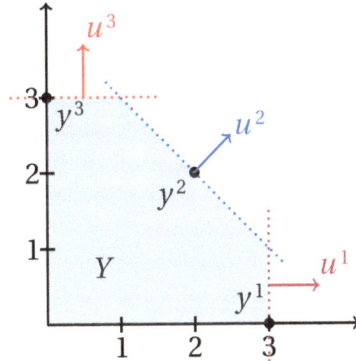

(a) Utility functions   (b) Illustration

Figure 2.2 A convex Y-equilibrium with a non-egalitarian Pareto-optimal outcome.

Let $y^1 = (3,0)$, $y^2 = (2,2)$ and $y^3 = (0,3)$ (Figure 2.2., panel (b)). The allocation (y^i) is Pareto-optimal: If (z^i) Pareto-dominates (y^i), then $z_1^i + z_2^i \geq y_1^i + y_2^i$ for all i with at least one inequality. Thus, $\Sigma_i(z_1^i + z_2^i) > \Sigma(y_1^i + y_2^i) = 10$, which is not feasible. The set Y is the intersection of (H^i) where each H^i is a half-space of bundles below i's indifference curve, which includes y^i.

The pair $\langle Y, (y^i) \rangle$ is a convex para-equilibrium and, by Proposition 2.4, (y^i) is a convex Y-equilibrium outcome. To see this directly, note that if there were a larger convex para-equilibrium, $\langle Z, (z^i) \rangle$, then Z would contain an element that is not in Y. Any such element is strictly preferred to y^i for at least one agent i. Thus, (z^i) would Pareto-dominate (y^i).

There can exist a non Pareto-optimal interior convex equilibrium outcome:

Consider the economy (depicted in Figure 2.3) with two agents, two goods, total bundle $e = (3,3)$, and kinked utility functions as depicted (a small deviation could make them strictly convex). Agent 1's indifference curve has slope -1.25, and agent 2's indifference curve has slope -0.8. The depicted allocation $y^1 = (2,1)$ and $y^2 = (1,2)$ is not Pareto-optimal since it is mutually beneficial to have agent 1 get one additional unit of good 1 and one unit fewer of good 2.

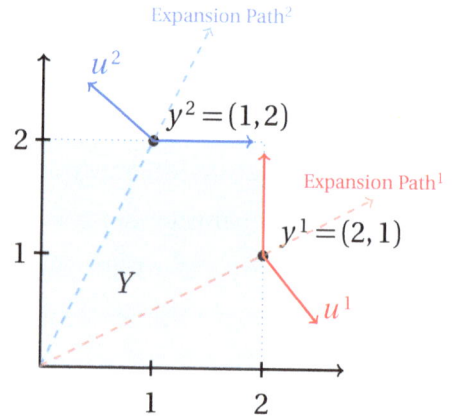

Figure 2.3 A non Pareto-optimal convex equilibrium.

The configuration $\langle Y, (y^i) \rangle$ is a convex para-equilibrium. In any larger convex para-equilibrium, $\langle Z, (z^i) \rangle$, the convex set Z includes a bundle that is strictly better for at least one of the agents and, therefore, $z^1 \neq y^1$ and $z^2 \neq y^2$. Given the agents' indifference curves, in z^1 agent 1 receives more of good 1 and less of good 2 than in y^1. Furthermore, agent 1 must not prefer another bundle on the line segment between z^1 and the corner $(2,2)$. This means that the slope between these two points has to be at least -1.25 or, in other words, $z_2^1 - 2 \geq -1.25 z_1^1 + 2.5$, which implies $z_2^1 + z_1^1 \geq 4.5 - 0.25 z_1^1 > 3$ where the last inequality is due to $3 \geq e_1 \geq z_1^1$. Likewise, agent 2's total demands are greater than 3, and such demands are infeasible.

Initial Endowments: Recall that a division economy differs from the standard exchange economy as it does not specify an initial distribution of the goods. One way to incorporate initial endowments into our framework is by the following notion of a *trade economy*. Let (e^i) be an initial endowment profile. Let $X = \mathbb{R}^m$ where a member of X is interpreted as a trade (and thus includes negative components as well). Set F to include all profiles of trades (t^i) such that $\Sigma_i t^i = 0$ and for every agent i, the post-trade bundle $t^i + e^i \geq 0$. As to the preferences, assume that each agent i has a basic preference relation $\succsim_c^i$ over the set of bundles (satisfying the standard division economy assumptions). Among trades that give an agent a non-negative amount of every good, agent i's preferences $\succsim^i$ on X are induced from their basic preferences by $t^i \succsim^i s^i$ if $t^i + e^i \succsim_c^i s^i + e^i$. Every agent prefers the no-exchange option 0 to any trade which leaves them with a negative amount of any good.

Analogous results to the previous claims for the division economy also hold for the trade economy: (i) the profile of trades in any competitive equilibrium in the standard exchange economy is a convex Y-equilibrium outcome in this trade economy, and (ii) any Pareto-optimal convex Y-equilibrium outcome in the trade economy, where at least one agent has a strictly positive post-trade allocation, is a profile of trades in a competitive equilibrium of the standard exchange economy.

2.9   The Give-and-Take Economy

Recall that in the give-and-take economy, the set of alternatives is $X = [-1, 1]$, where a positive x represents a withdrawal of x from a social fund while a negative x represents a contribution of $-x$. Feasibility requires that the social fund be balanced, that is, $(x^i) \in F$ iff $\Sigma_i x^i = 0$. All agents have strictly convex preferences over X with agent i's ideal denoted by $peak^i$. As mentioned earlier, the give-and-take economy is an economic situation in which the market plays no role. We will see that norms regarding what is permissible and what is forbidden can serve as an effective non-market tool for achieving harmony.

The case $\Sigma_i peak^i = 0$ is "bliss": everything is permitted and $\langle X, (peak^i) \rangle$ is a convex Y-equilibrium. However, in general, there is tension between feasibility and the agents' desires. The following claim characterizes the convex Y-equilibrium for the case where the sum of what people ideally want to take is greater than what people ideally want to give. We will see now that, in this case, there is a unique convex Y-equilibrium. In it, people are allowed to give as much as they want but there is a bound on the maximum that can be taken, and its outcome is Pareto optimal.

Claim: A Characterization of the Convex Y-equilibrium

Consider a give-and-take economy with $\Sigma peak^i > 0$. There is a unique convex Y-equilibrium $\langle Y, (y^i) \rangle$. The set Y takes the form $[-1, m]$ for some $m > 0$, and (y^i) is Pareto optimal.

Proof:

Consider a permissible set of the form $[-1, m]$. If $m < 0$, then all agents must give. If $m \geq 0$, then every agent who wants to give will select his peak, and every agent who wants to take is either at his peak or has a peak to the right of m and makes do with taking m. Let $D(m)$ be the sum of all agents' choices given the permissible set $[-1, m]$. The function D is continuous, strictly increasing for any m smaller than $\max\{peak^i\}$, and is constant with value $\Sigma_i peak^i > 0$ for any larger m. In particular, $D(0) \leq 0$ and $D(1) > 0$. Thus, there is a unique $m^* \geq 0$ for which $D(m^*) = 0$.

The permissible set $[-1, m^*]$, together with the agents' optimal choices from that set, constitutes a convex para-equilibrium. It is also a convex Y-equilibrium because there is no convex para-equilibrium with a larger permissible set. If there were, it would have the form $[-1, m]$ where $m > m^*$, but then agents would take too much (since $D(m) > 0$).

The profile (y^i) is Pareto optimal: For each i, y^i is at or to the left of his peak. Thus, if $(z^i) \in F$ Pareto-dominates (y^i), then $y^i \leq z^i$ for all i with at least one strict inequality, thus $0 = \Sigma y^i < \Sigma z^i$, violating feasibility.

To prove uniqueness of the convex equilibrium, it remains to be shown that any closed convex para-equilibrium permissible set $[x, y]$ is included in $[-1, m^*]$. In order for the social fund to be balanced, it must be that $x \leq 0 \leq y$. In equilibrium, agents who wish to give will do so at either their peak or at x if $peak^i < x$. Therefore, the total giving in $[x, y]$ is not more than that in $[-1, m^*]$. Since the social fund is balanced, the total taking in $[x, y]$ must also be less than or equal to that in $[-1, m^*]$, and therefore $y \leq m^*$. Thus, $[x, y] \subseteq [-1, m^*]$.

Comment: For this economy, while convex Y-equilibria are Pareto-optimal, a Y-equilibrium outcome need not be. A detailed example appears in Richter and Rubinstein (2020). The essence of the example is as follows: Let $X = \{-2, -1, 0, 1, 2\}$ and $n = 2$. The agents' "convex" preference relations are $1 \succ^1 0 \succ^1 -1 \succ^1 -2 \succ^1 2$ and $1 \succ^2 2 \succ^2 0 \succ^2 -1 \succ^2 -2$. The "convex" permissible set $Y = \{-2, -1, 0\}$, together with the profile $y^1 = y^2 = 0$, is a "convex" Y-equilibrium with a Pareto-optimal outcome. However, it is easy to verify that the non-convex permissible set $Y = \{-2, 2\}$ with the profile $y^1 = -2, y^2 = 2$ is a Y-equilibrium whose outcome is Pareto dominated by $z^1 = -1, z^2 = 1$.

2.10 The Stay Close Economy

The stay close economy is a convex Euclidean economy in which X is a closed convex set of locations and F is the set of profiles for which the distance between any two agents is at most d^*. That is, each member of the group chooses a position (for example, a political stance or a geographical location), and the group's survival requires that the members "stay close" to each other. As always, each agent has strictly convex preferences for his own location without regard to the location of others. The potential source of conflict is that the group members have a diverse set of ideal locations which fails the closeness requirement. Note that the set F satisfies the imitation condition defined in Section 2.3. When $d^* = 0$, this economy is called a *consensus economy*.

In a centralized society, the authorities can coerce agents into occupying locations that guarantee survival. In a market, members would have to pay each other to stay close by. The Y-equilibrium idea is that there are norms that determine the borders of the permissible locations and strike a balance between societal harmony and individual liberty. Each agent chooses his most preferred location within the borders, and the outcome is that they all live close enough to one another. The borders are maximally liberal in the sense that if the borders are enlarged in any way, then the resulting individual choices would not be "close enough".

A modified serial dictatorship provides a simple method for finding a Pareto-optimal profile and proving its existence: agent 1 selects his ideal point $x^1 = peak^1$ in X, then agent 2 selects his most preferred point from among those that are "close enough" to x^1, and each subsequent agent i selects his most preferred point x^i from among those which are "close enough" to all of those previously selected, that is, $\{x \mid d(x, x^j) \leq d^*,$ for every $j < i\}$.

The following claim establishes that every Pareto-optimal profile is both a Y-equilibrium outcome and a convex Y-equilibrium outcome. As a partial converse, it also shows that Y-equilibrium outcomes are Pareto optimal; however, convex Y-equilibrium outcomes may or may not be.

Claim: Pareto Optimality and Y-equilibrium

For a stay close economy:

(i) A Y-equilibrium and a convex Y-equilibrium exist. Moreover, any Pareto-optimal allocation is both a Y-equilibrium outcome and a convex Y-equilibrium outcome.

(ii) Every Y-equilibrium outcome is Pareto optimal. However, a convex Y-equilibrium outcome need not be.

(iii) If X is a subset of a one-dimensional Euclidean space, then any convex Y-equilibrium outcome is Pareto optimal.

Proof:

(i) The modified serial dictatorship algorithm above establishes the existence of Pareto-optimal allocations. Given a Pareto-optimal allocation (y^i), let Y be the convex hull of $\{y^1, \ldots, y^n\}$. Any point $\Sigma_j \lambda_j y^j$ in Y is at most d^* away from every y^i since $d(\Sigma_j \lambda_j y^j, y^i) \leq \Sigma_j \lambda_j d(y^j, y^i) \leq \Sigma_j \lambda_j d^* \leq d^*$ (the first inequality is due to the triangle inequality). Each y^i is $\succsim^i$-maximal in Y since any agent moving to another location in Y preserves feasibility and (y^i) is Pareto optimal. Therefore, $\langle Y, (y^i) \rangle$ is a convex para-equilibrium. By Proposition 2.1, (y^i) is a Y-equilibrium profile and, by Proposition 2.4, it is also a convex Y-equilibrium profile.

(ii) Since F satisfies the imitation property, by Proposition 2.2, any Y-equilibrium outcome is Pareto optimal. The following economy shows that a convex Y-equilibrium can be non Pareto-optimal: Let $n = 2$, $d^* = 0$, $X = \mathbb{R}^2$, and agents' preferences be given by $U^1(x_1, x_2) = 2x_2 - (x_2 - x_1)^2$ and $U^2(x_1, x_2) = 2x_2 - (x_2 + x_1)^2$ (see Figure 2.4). From $Y = \{(x_1, x_2) \mid x_2 \leq 0\}$, both agents choose $y^1 = y^2 = (0,0)$ and the pair $\langle Y, (y^i) \rangle$ is a convex para-equilibrium. If there were a larger convex para-equilibrium set, then there

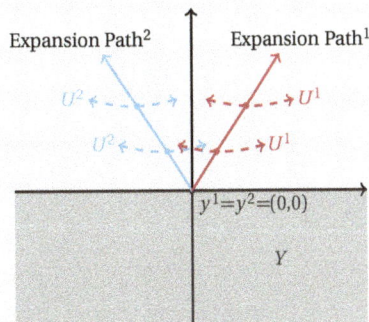

Figure 2.4 Non Pareto-optimal convex equilibrium in a consensus economy

would be one of the form $Z = \{(x_1, x_2) \mid x_2 \leq z\}$ with $z > 0$. From Z, agent 1 prefers (z, z) and agent 2 prefers $(-z, z)$, and this profile is not in F. The equilibrium outcome is not Pareto optimal since both agents prefer $(0, 1)$ to $(0, 0)$. This example can be easily modified for any $d^* > 0$ by setting $Y = \{(x_1, x_2) \mid x_2 \leq d^*/2\}$, $y^1 = (d^*/2, d^*/2)$ and $y^2 = (-d^*/2, d^*/2)$.

(iii) Let $\langle Y, (y^i) \rangle$ be a convex Y-equilibrium, L be the minimum of the agents' peaks, R be the maximum, $\underline{y} = \min_i y^i$, and $\overline{y} = \max_i y^i$.

If $R - L \leq d^*$, then $Y = X$ and every agent chooses his peak, which is obviously a Pareto-optimal outcome.

If $R - L > d^*$, then it must be that $\overline{y} - \underline{y} = d^*$, since otherwise $\overline{y} - \underline{y} < d^*$, and there is an agent who is not at his peak. Thus, his choice must be on the boundary of Y. This boundary can be slightly enlarged and the profile of agents' new optimal choices will be feasible.

By the convexity of Y, each agent who chooses $\overline{y}$ is at his peak or wants to move to the right, each agent who chooses $\underline{y}$ is at his peak or wants to move to the left, and the others choose their peaks. Thus, any profile that Pareto dominates (y^i) must increase the maximum distance between agents, which violates feasibility since $\overline{y} - \underline{y} = d^*$.

3 Status and Indoctrination

We now turn to a different notion of economic harmony studied in Richter and Rubinstein (2015). As always in this book, an equilibrium is a *profile* of alternatives (one for each agent) and an additional parameter. Here, the parameter is a commonly accepted ordering on the set of all alternatives that affects the choices agents can make. We refer to it as a *public ordering*.

We have in mind three interpretations of a public ordering:

Values. When the alternatives are objects, the public ordering may reflect their "value" or "worth". A holder of an object can exchange it for any lower-valued object, but not for a higher-valued one. This interpretation aligns with the standard notion of the "more expensive" relation — a holder of a bundle in a market can exchange it for a cheaper one, but not for a more expensive one.

Prestige. When the alternatives are positions in a society, the public ordering may reflect the prestige of these positions. According to this interpretation, an agent can exchange his position for any less prestigious one, but not a more prestigious one.

Under the above two interpretations, society restricts an agent's *ability* to replace the alternative he has. He can only move "down" to a "less valuable" or "less prestigious" one, but not "up". In contrast, in the next interpretation, the public ordering's meaning is reversed: lower-ranked alternatives are more "valuable" for society.

Indoctrination. Agents are indoctrinated by society regarding the interests of society as a whole. A public ordering inversely ranks the alternatives according to their benefit to society: the lower ranked an alternative is, the more beneficial it is to society. An agent is only willing to replace his assigned alternative with one that is better for society (i.e. lower-ranked by the public ordering). The indoctrination does not affect the agent's basic preferences (in

©2024 Michael Richter and Ariel Rubinstein, CC BY-NC-ND 4.0   https://doi.org/10.11647/OBP.0404.03

contrast to the biased preferences model discussed in Chapter 4) but, rather, modifies his choice set. An agent only considers moving from one alternative to another if it benefits society (and will only make such a move if he also personally benefits).

With the above interpretations in mind, we will discuss two types of equilibria, which fit into the two categories of equilibrium discussed in Section 0.4. The first is the *status equilibrium*: it is a feasible profile of choices and a public ordering such that no agent strictly prefers any alternative that is weakly lower-ranked by the public ordering than the one assigned to him. Thus, the public ordering limits the agents' deviations from the equilibrium profile: an agent who is assigned an alternative only considers deviating to alternatives that are weakly lower-ranked (by the public ordering) than the one he is assigned. Deviations are purely self-serving and contemplated without regard to feasibility.

In the taxonomy of Section 0.4, the status equilibrium belongs to the deviation group (like Nash equilibrium). In the last section of the chapter, we will study the *initial status equilibrium* concept, which fits into the choice group (like competitive equilibrium). This concept operates on an extended economy (in which the model of an economy is extended to include an initial profile). In the initial profile, each agent is assigned an alternative that he can always choose and which, together with the public ordering, determine the agent's choice set. An initial status equilibrium consists of a feasible profile and a public ordering, but this time the profile of choices must be such that no agent strictly prefers any alternative that is weakly lower-ranked by the public ordering than the one initially assigned to him. Thus, the public ordering limits an agent's choice set: he only considers alternatives that are weakly lower-ranked than his initial alternative.

3.1 Status Equilibrium

Definition: Status Equilibrium

Given an economy $\langle N, X, (\succsim^i)_{i \in N}, F \rangle$, a **status equilibrium** is a pair $\langle P, (x^i)_{i \in N} \rangle$ where $(x^i)_{i \in N}$ is a profile and P is an ordering (a complete, reflexive, and transitive binary relation) on X satisfying:

Feasibility: the profile (x^i) is in F.

Personal optimality: for every agent i, the element x^i is $\succsim^i$-maximal in $\{z \in X \mid x^i P z\}$.

The ordering P is referred to as a **public ordering**.

As mentioned, under the first two interpretations of a public ordering, it ranks the alternatives by value or prestige. The term $a P b$ means that *a is more expensive than b* or that *a is more prestigious than b*. An equilibrium public ordering stabilizes the equilibrium profile in the sense that every agent is satisfied with his assignment *given* that he is bounded by the worth (or prestige) of his assigned alternative. Under the third interpretation, P is a social motive that systematically affects an agent's willingness to exchange his assigned alternative. The term $a P b$ means that "*a is less socially desirable than b*" (this is not a mistake... *less* and not *more*). If an agent i is assigned x^i, then he cannot bear the idea of exchanging it for an alternative that is less socially desirable and, therefore, he only considers more socially desirable alternatives (i.e. those which are lower-ranked by P). Under this interpretation, an equilibrium consists of a public ordering and a feasible profile in which no agent both: i) wishes to exchange his assigned alternative, according to his personal preferences and ii) is able to justify the exchange as furthering society's interests, according to the public ordering.

Proposition 3.1: A Second Welfare Theorem

Any Pareto-optimal profile is a status equilibrium profile.

Proof:

Let (a^i) be a Pareto-optimal profile. Define the binary relation D on $A = \{a^1, \ldots, a^n\}$ by xDy if x is desired by a holder of y, that is, there are i and j such that $x = a^i \succ^j a^j = y$. If D has a cycle, then there is a set of agents who can permute their alternatives among themselves (recall that F is closed under permutations) so that all of them are strictly better off, contradicting (a^i) being Pareto-optimal. Since D has no cycles, it can be extended to a complete ordering over A. Then, D can be extended to a strict ordering P on the entire set X by putting all elements in $X - A$ above all elements in A (making all unassigned elements "unaffordable") and arbitrarily ranking the elements in $X - A$ among themselves. Personal optimality holds since, for every agent i, the alternative a^i is optimal in $\{x \mid a^i Px\}$ (if $a^i Px$, then $x = a^j$ for some j, and if i were to prefer it, then xDa^i, which contradicts $a^i Px$ since P extends D).

By the same proof, any feasible profile (Pareto-optimal or not) for which the relation D does not have cycles is a status equilibrium profile. In particular, in the consensus economy, where all agents have to make the same choice, any profile that assigns the same element x^* to all agents is supported by any public ordering that ranks x^* as the unique lowest element in X and thus all other alternatives are "blocked". Such a profile might be not Pareto-optimal. Thus, any Pareto-optimal profile is a status equilibrium profile, but a status equilibrium profile does not have to be Pareto-optimal.

3.2 Status Equilibrium – Examples

Example: The Jobs Economy

Let X be a non-singleton set of types of jobs. Each agent holds *strict* preferences on X. Feasibility is given by a vector $(n_x)_{x \in X}$ where n_x is the number of available jobs of type x (non-emptiness of F requires that $\Sigma_{x \in X} n_x \geq n$).

A public ordering in this example has a natural interpretation of social status, which is often associated with a job. Once an agent is assigned to a job, he cannot switch to a higher-status job but he can switch to any job of equal or lower status (e.g. a professor can move to a lower-ranked university but not to a higher-ranked one). The housing model of Shapley and Scarf (1974) is the special case where $n_x \equiv 1$ and $|X| = n$.

Claim: The following holds for the jobs economy:

(i) If $\Sigma_x n_x = n$, then the First Welfare Theorem holds: every status equilibrium profile is Pareto-optimal.

(ii) If $\Sigma_x n_x > n$, then the First Welfare Theorem fails: there is always a status equilibrium profile that is not Pareto-optimal.

Proof: (i) Let $\langle P, (x^i) \rangle$ be a status equilibrium. Assume by contradiction that the feasible profile (y^i) Pareto-dominates (x^i). Let j be an agent for whom x^j is P-maximal from among $\{x^i \mid y^i \neq x^i\}$. Since preferences are strict, it must be that $y^j \succ^j x^j$ and, therefore, $y^j P x^j$. Since $\Sigma_x n_x = n$, it must be that in any feasible profile, all jobs are filled. Therefore, there is another agent whose original job is y^j and whose new job is not, contradicting the P-maximality of x^j from among $\{x^i \mid y^i \neq x^i\}$.

(ii) Let (x^i) be a Pareto-optimal profile. By Proposition 3.1, there is a public ordering such that $\langle P, (x^i) \rangle$ is a status equilibrium. Let z denote a job with spare capacity, and let j be an agent who does not have job z (which exists since $\Sigma_x n_x > n$ and $|X| > 1$). Let (y^i) be the feasible profile obtained from (x^i) by moving j from x^j to z. Since (x^i) is Pareto-optimal, every agent who does not have job z strictly prefers his assigned job to z and thus, (y^i) is not Pareto-optimal. Let P' be the public ordering obtained from P by moving z to the bottom rank. The pair $\langle P', (y^i) \rangle$ is clearly a status equilibrium.

Example: *R*-Monotonic Preferences

Let R be a strict partial ordering (irreflexive, transitive, and anti-symmetric but not necessarily complete) on X. A preference relation $\succsim$ is R-**monotonic** if $a \succ b$ whenever aRb. For example, let X be a set of bundles and R be defined by xRy if the bundle x contains weakly more than y of every good and strictly more of at least one. In this case, R-monotonicity is the standard notion of strong monotonicity.

It will now be shown that, for any economy with R-monotonic preferences, any status equilibrium profile can also be supported as a status equilibrium with an R-monotonic public ordering. Thus, a stronger assumption on agents' preferences (R-monotonicity) leads to stronger conclusions about the equilibrium public ordering (being R-monotonic).

Claim: Let R be a strict partial ordering and let $\langle N, X, (\succsim^i)_{i \in N}, F \rangle$ be an economy where every preference $\succsim^i$ is R-monotonic. If $\langle P, (x^i)_{i \in N} \rangle$ is a status equilibrium, then there is an R-monotonic ordering Q such that $\langle Q, (x^i)_{i \in N} \rangle$ is also a status equilibrium.

Proof: Define the *desire* binary relation D as yDz if there is an agent who is assigned z and strictly prefers y (and thus, it must be that yPz strictly). Let $S = R \cup D$. The relation S is acyclic: if not, let $z_1 S_1 z_2 S_2 z_3 S_3 \ldots z_m S_m z_1$ be a minimal cycle where each S_i is either R or D.

- It cannot be that all S_i are R because R is acyclic.
- It cannot be that all S_i are D since $z_{i-1} D z_i$ implies $z_{i-1} P z_i$ strictly and thus, a D-cycle implies a strict P-cycle, which is impossible.
- It cannot be that the cycle $S_1, \ldots, S_m$ contains both D and R. This is because, if it did, then it would contain an R followed by a D. However, if $aRbDc$, then there is a j such that $c = x^j$ and $b \succ^j c$. Since $\succ^j$ extends R, it follows that $a \succ^j b$ and therefore, $a \succ^j c$ and so aDc. Therefore, the cycle can be shortened.

Thus, S is a strict partial ordering. Extend S to an ordering Q. Since S extends R, so does Q and thus, Q is R-monotonic. Since S extends D, so does Q and thus, $\langle Q, (x^i) \rangle$ is a status equilibrium.

3.3 A Detour: Convex Preferences

In Section 3.4, we will refine the notion of a status equilibrium by imposing some structure to the public ordering. In preparation, we make a detour to the concept of convex preferences.

One conventional definition of convex preferences for Euclidean spaces requires that if a is weakly preferred to b, then any convex combination of a and b is also weakly preferred to b. This definition is equivalent to requiring that all upper contours (sets of the type $\{x \mid x \succ a\}$) are convex sets. Both of these definitions refer to the term "convex combination", which itself uses an algebraic structure on the space of alternatives and so does not apply to economies where the set X lacks such a structure.

Following Richter and Rubinstein (2019), we suggest an alternative definition of convex preferences which generalizes the standard Euclidean notion and is also applicable to spaces without algebraic structure. A cornerstone of this approach is the view that preferences are built from primitive building blocks. Here, we take the building blocks to be the members of a set of orderings Λ, which we call *primitive orderings*. Each primitive ordering is a complete, reflexive, and transitive binary relation over the set X (indifferences are allowed). We interpret the primitive orderings as expressions of objective attributes of the alternatives that are in the vocabulary of all agents.

The assumption behind this definition is that, when thinking about replacing an alternative $b \in X$, an agent has in mind a necessary criterion (primitive ordering) that is *critical*, in the sense that, for an alternative to be better than b, it must be better by this criterion. Note that the critical criterion can depend on b.

For example, imagine a department chair who is contemplating replacing b, who is a weak teacher. In this case, the critical consideration may be pedagogical ability, and any teacher who is pedagogically worse than b will be rejected. However, this does not mean that any candidate who is pedagogically better than b will be preferred. Again, the critical criterion can vary from one alternative to another: when the department chair considers replacing c, who is a great teacher and a poor researcher, he may feel that research ability is now critical, and thus, any candidate who is a worse researcher than c will be judged to be a worse candidate than c.

Definition: Λ-convex Preferences

Let X be a set of objects and Λ be a set of orderings on X referred to as **primitive orderings**. The symbol $\vartriangleright$ represents a generic member of Λ. A preference relation $\succsim$ on X is **Λ-convex** if:

   $\forall b \in X, \exists \vartriangleright \in \Lambda$ such that for $x \neq b$ it is necessary for $x \succ b$ that $x \vartriangleright b$.

A preference relation $\succsim$ on X is **Λ-strictly convex** if:

   $\forall\, b \in X, \exists \vartriangleright \in \Lambda$ such that for $x \neq b$ it is necessary for $x \succsim b$ that $x \vartriangleright b$.

In both definitions, the ordering $\vartriangleright$ is called a **critical direction** at b (there can be multiple critical directions).

Three comments:

(i) Every (strict) primitive ordering in Λ is Λ-(strictly) convex: for each alternative, the primitive ordering itself is a critical direction.

(ii) A "Pareto" property holds: If b and c are distinct, $b \vartriangleright c$ for every $\vartriangleright \in \Lambda$, and $\succsim$ is Λ-convex, then $b \succsim c$. This is because there is a critical ordering $\vartriangleright$ attached to b and $b \vartriangleright c$ and therefore, c cannot be strictly preferred to b. For Λ-strictly convex preferences, the conclusion is stronger, namely, $b \succ c$.

(iii) In Richter and Rubinstein (2019), we also suggested other similar definitions of convex preferences and discussed their connection to Edelman and Jamison (1985)'s notion of "abstract convexity".

Underpinning our convexity notion is the abstraction of a concept that plays a fundamental role in economic analysis when we talk about convex preferences on a Euclidean space: for each alternative, there is a *hyperplane* which contains it, such that all weakly preferred alternatives lie on one side of the hyperplane. In the same spirit, our notion of convex preferences requires that for every alternative there is an *ordering* that puts all preferred alternatives on one side of the ordering.

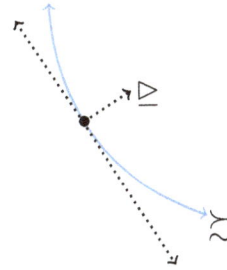

Figure 3.1 A supporting hyperplane and its corresponding critical direction

The definition of convex preferences is attractive for several reasons:

(a) It is compelling as a procedural assumption of preference formation.

(b) It emphasizes and allows for the dependence of the convexity property on the specification of the considerations used to construct preferences.

(c) It generalizes standard convexity for Euclidean spaces, as will be shown later.

(d) It does not require any algebraic structure.

Example: Left and Right

Let $X = [0,1]$, and suppose that Λ contains two orderings: the rightist $\unrhd_R$ (which ranks elements to the right higher) and the leftist $\unrhd_L$ (which ranks elements to the left higher). A preference relation is *single-peaked* if:

(i) it has a unique maximum point (*peak*) in X; and

(ii) it is strictly increasing below the peak and strictly decreasing above it.

Claim: Let $\Lambda = \{\unrhd_L, \unrhd_R\}$ and $X = [0,1]$. A continuous preference relation is Λ-strictly convex if and only if it is single-peaked.

Proof: Suppose $\succsim$ is singled-peaked. At any $b > peak$, the ordering $\unrhd_L$ is critical, while at any $b < peak$ the ordering $\unrhd_R$ is critical. At the peak, both orderings are critical.

Suppose $\succsim$ is Λ-strictly convex. Since the preferences are continuous and X is compact, there is a $\succsim$-maximal element. It is unique since if there are two $\succsim$-maximal elements $y < z$, and x is between y and z, then $y \rhd_L x$ and $z \rhd_R x$ and both y and z are weakly preferred to x. Therefore, there is no critical direction at x.

Let M be the $\succsim$-maximal element. For every $y < x < M$, the critical ordering at x must be $\rhd_R$ and thus $y \prec x$. Therefore, $\succsim$ is strictly increasing to the left of M. Likewise, for every $x > M$, the critical ordering must be $\rhd_L$, and $\succsim$ is strictly decreasing to the right of M. Thus, the preferences are single-peaked with the peak at M. ∎

The next example shows that, for continuous preferences, the Λ-convexity notion used here generalizes the standard notion of convex preferences on Euclidean spaces.

Example: Euclidean Space with Algebraic Linear Orderings

Let X be an open convex subset of a Euclidean space. For any vector $v \neq 0$, define the *algebraic linear ordering* $\geq_v$ by $x \geq_v y$ if $v \cdot x \geq v \cdot y$. Let Ψ be the set of all algebraic linear orderings.

Claim: Let $\succsim$ be a continuous preference relation on X. Then: $\succsim$ is convex by the standard definition if and only if $\succsim$ is Ψ-convex.

Proof: Assume $\succsim$ is convex by the standard definition. That is, for every $b \in X$, the set $U_\succ(b) = \{z \mid z \succ b\}$ is convex. Since $\succsim$ is continuous, by the separating hyperplane theorem, there exists $\geq_v \in \Psi$ such that for every $x \in U_\succ(b)$ it holds that $x >_v b$. That is, $\geq_v$ is a critical direction.

Assume $\succsim$ is Ψ-convex. Let a, c be elements in X such that $a, c \succ b$, and let z be an element on the line between a and c. By Ψ-convexity, there is a critical direction $\geq_v$ at z. Then, $z \geq_v a$ or $z \geq_v c$ or both, and since $\succsim$ is Ψ-convex, it follows that $z \succsim a$ or $z \succsim c$, and thus $z \succ b$. ∎

Construction of Convex Preferences: For a finite set X, if all orderings in Λ are strict, then the following procedure builds a Λ-convex preference relation: Take an alternative x_1 which is at the bottom of one of the primitive orderings, and place it at the bottom of $\succsim$. Then, let x_2 be an alternative at the bottom of $X - \{x_1\}$ with respect to one of the primitive orderings, and place it (strongly or weakly) above x_1. Continue this procedure until all alternatives are exhausted. The constructed preference is Λ-convex since the position of each $b \in X$ in $\succsim$ was determined when b was at the bottom of some primitive ordering, which is then a critical direction at b since any strictly preferred alternative is ranked strictly higher than b by that ordering.

If X is finite and all orderings in Λ are strict, then every Λ-convex preference relation $\succsim$ can be constructed by the procedure described above (see Richter and Rubinstein (2019)): To apply the construction to obtain $\succsim$, at every stage we must identify an alternative and a primitive ordering $\unrhd$ so that the alternative is both $\succsim$-minimal and $\unrhd$-minimal from among the remaining alternatives. To start, pick $x \in X$ which is $\succsim$-minimal, and let $\unrhd \in \Lambda$ be a critical direction at x. If x is $\unrhd$-minimal, then set $x_1 = x$. If not, then pick y which is minimal according to the same $\unrhd$. The alternative y is also $\succsim$-minimal since $\unrhd$ is a critical direction at x and $x \unrhd y$, and then set $x_1 = y$. Continue inductively with the remaining alternatives.

Utility Representation: We say that a preference relation $\succsim$ over X has a Λ-*maxmin representation* if there is a profile of functions $(U_\unrhd)_{\unrhd \in \Lambda}$ such that for every $\unrhd \in \Lambda$ the function $U_\unrhd$ is a utility representation of $\unrhd$ and the function $U(x) = \min_\unrhd U_\unrhd(x)$ is well-defined and represents $\succsim$.

If Λ is finite and $\succsim$ has a Λ-maxmin representation $(U_\unrhd)$, then $\succsim$ is Λ-convex: For any $b \in X$, take the ordering $\unrhd \in \Lambda$ for which $U_\unrhd(b)$ is minimal. The ordering $\unrhd$ is a critical direction at b because $b \unrhd x$ implies $U_\unrhd(b) \geq U_\unrhd(x)$ and thus, $U(b) \geq U(x)$ and $b \succsim x$. In Richter and Rubinstein (2019), it is shown that for finite X, the converse is also true: any Λ-strictly convex preference relation has a Λ-maxmin representation.

The existence of such a representation means that we can identify every alternative in the set X by a vector of numbers in $\mathbb{R}^\Lambda$ such that:

(i) for every primitive ordering, the values that are attached to the elements in X at the corresponding coordinate are consistent with that primitive ordering's ranking; and

(ii) the preferences are represented by the minimum value attached to an alternative across the different dimensions.

3.4   Primitive Equilibrium

In the canonical consumer model, the set of alternatives (bundles) is a subset of a Euclidean space and the following holds:

(i) Agents have standard convex preferences.
(ii) The "more expensive than" ordering is induced by a linear price system.

   In the language of this chapter:

(i) Agents have Ψ-convex preferences where Ψ is the set of all algebraic linear orderings (as shown in Section 3.3).
(ii) The "more expensive than" ordering $\geq_p$ on the set of alternatives (defined by $x \geq_p y$ if $p \cdot x \geq p \cdot y$) is a member of Ψ.

An important point is that the same set of primitive orderings appears in (i) and (ii) above. This suggests two new definitions. First, we enrich the notion of an economy with a set of primitives orderings Λ and require that all agents' preference relations are Λ-convex. We refer to such an economy by the term *convex economy*. Second, we refine the status equilibrium notion and require that the public ordering is one of the primitive orderings in Λ. We refer to such an equilibrium as a *primitive equilibrium*. Formally:

Definition: Convex Economy

A **convex economy** is a tuple $\langle N, X, (\succsim^i)_{i \in N}, F, \Lambda \rangle$ where $\langle N, X, (\succsim^i)_{i \in N}, F \rangle$ is an economy, Λ is a set of primitive orderings over X, and all preferences are Λ-convex.

Definition: Primitive Equilibrium

Let $\langle N, X, (\succsim^i)_{i \in N}, F, \Lambda \rangle$ be a convex economy. A **primitive equilibrium** is a status equilibrium $\langle \trianglerighteq, (x^i)_{i \in N} \rangle$ where $\trianglerighteq \in \Lambda$.

Obviously, any primitive equilibrium is a status equilibrium, and when Λ is the set of all orderings, any status equilibrium is a primitive equilibrium.

Example: The Give-and-Take Convex Economy

We return to the give-and-take economy. Recall that $X = [-1, 1]$ and F is the set of all profiles that sum up to 0. Let Λ consist of the two natural orderings: the rightist $\trianglerighteq_R$ (which favours taking) and the leftist $\trianglerighteq_L$ (which favours giving). Assume that every agent i holds continuous Λ-strictly convex preferences (with a single peak denoted by $peak^i$).

When $\Sigma_i peak^i = 0$, there is no conflict of interest in the economy and either primitive ordering, together with all agents choosing their peaks, is a primitive equilibrium. In fact, these are the only primitive equilibria (if $\langle \trianglerighteq_L, (x^i)_{i \in N} \rangle$ is an equilibrium, then $peak^i \leq x^i$ for all i and therefore, $x^i = peak^i$ for all i).

A more interesting case is $\Sigma_i peak^i > 0$ where agents wish to take more than they wish to give. Let $F_\leq$ be the set of all feasible profiles with all agents at or to the left of their peaks. We now verify that $F_\leq$ is equal to the set of all Pareto-optimal profiles. Any $(x^i) \in F_\leq$ is Pareto-optimal because any profile (y^i) that Pareto-dominates it must rank $x^i \leq y^i$ for all i, with at least one strict inequality; however, such a profile is infeasible because $0 = \Sigma x^i < \Sigma y^i$. On the other hand, if (x^i) is feasible and not in $F_\leq$, then $peak^i < x^i$ for some agent i and, by the assumption that $\Sigma_i peak^i > 0$, there is an agent j for whom $x^j < peak^j$. Transferring some small amount from i (who takes too much) to j (who gives too much) would be a feasible Pareto improvement. The following claim shows that the First and Second Welfare Theorems hold for this example.

Claim: In the give-and-take convex economy with $\Sigma_i peak^i > 0$, the primitive equilibria are all tuples $\langle \trianglerighteq_R, (x^i)_{i \in N} \rangle$ where (x^i) is a Pareto-optimal profile.

Proof: A pair $\langle \trianglerighteq_L, (x^i)_{i \in N} \rangle$ cannot be a primitive equilibrium since then $peak^i \leq x^i$ for all i and thus $0 < \Sigma_i peak^i \leq \Sigma_i x^i$. If $\langle \trianglerighteq_R, (x^i)_{i \in N} \rangle$, is a primitive equilibrium, then (x^i) is in $F_\leq$, hence Pareto-optimal. Obviously, any pair $\langle \trianglerighteq_R, (x^i)_{i \in N} \rangle$ where (x^i) is in $F_\leq$ is a primitive equilibrium.   ■

The rightist ordering reflects the norm that an agent should not take more (or not give less) than his assignment. This is a reasonable norm for governing a voluntary public fund in a society where the "aggregate" tendency of agents is to take rather than give. Under the alternative interpretation of status, the public is indoctrinated with the idea that giving less or taking more than expected is shameful.

Example: The Consensus Economy

In this example, different political positions are represented by points on a line. The (finite or infinite) set $X \subseteq \mathbb{R}$ consists of all possible political positions. As in the previous example, the set of primitive orderings Λ consists of the rightist and the leftist orderings, and every agent i has a continuous and Λ-strictly convex preference relation with a peak denoted by $peak^i$. Denote by l the leftmost peak and by r the rightmost peak, and assume that $-1 < l < r < 1$. Harmony requires consensus, and thus F is the set of all constant profiles. The set of Pareto-optimal profiles consists of all profiles $(x^*, \ldots, x^*)$ with $x^* \in [l, r]$.

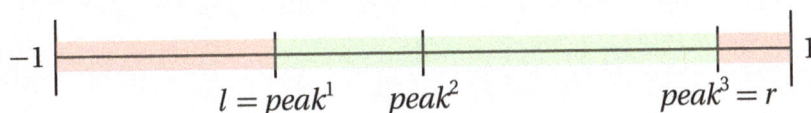

Figure 3.2 Primitive equilibrium positions – red; Pareto-optimal positions – green

The pair $\langle \trianglerighteq_L, (x^*, \ldots, x^*) \rangle$ is a primitive equilibrium if and only if $r \le x^*$. Likewise, the pair $\langle \trianglerighteq_R, (x^*, \ldots, x^*) \rangle$ is a primitive equilibrium if and only if $x^* \le l$. Therefore, except for the boundaries, the primitive equilibrium profiles and the Pareto-optimal profiles are almost completely disjoint. Thus, the First and Second Welfare Theorems both fail for this economy.

Example: A Convex Economy with No Primitive Equilibrium

Primitive equilibria can fail to exist even when a status equilibrium exists. Consider the convex housing economy with four agents and four houses arranged on a line $a--b--c--d$, with $\Lambda = \{\trianglerighteq_L, \trianglerighteq_R\}$. Agents 1 and 2 hold the preferences $\trianglerighteq_L$, while 3 and 4 hold the preferences $\trianglerighteq_R$. A status equilibrium exists (for example, the profile (a, b, c, d) with the public ordering $a\,Pd\,Pb\,Pc$). However, there are no primitive equilibria since any primitive ordering bottom-ranks an extreme alternative z (which is either a or d) and since there are two agents who top-rank z, at least one of them is not assigned z and strictly prefers z, violating the definition of primitive equilibrium.

3.5 A First Welfare Theorem

We have just seen that the consensus economy has primitive equilibrium profiles that are not Pareto-optimal. The following are two other illuminating examples in which primitive equilibrium profiles can be non Pareto-optimal:

(i) In a single-agent convex economy, every feasible alternative x^* (preference-maximal or not) together with a critical direction of the preferences at x^* is a primitive equilibrium.

(ii) In a convex economy where all agents' preferences are equal to the same primitive ordering $\trianglerighteq$, every feasible profile (whether it is Pareto-optimal or not) combined with the public ordering $\trianglerighteq$ is a primitive equilibrium.

The following condition on *convex environments*, $\langle N, X, F, \Lambda \rangle$, plays a key role in explaining why the First Welfare Theorem is valid in the standard division economy but not in the above examples.

Definition: Condition D

A convex environment $\langle N, X, F, \Lambda \rangle$ satisfies **condition D** if there is no primitive ordering $\trianglerighteq$ and two distinct feasible profiles (a^i) and (b^i) such that $b^i \triangleright a^i$ or $b^i = a^i$ for all i.

Three prominent convex economies that satisfy condition D are: (i) the housing economy with any set of primitive orderings, (ii) the standard division economy with Λ being the set of all algebraic linear orderings and F requiring that all goods are fully allocated, and (iii) the give-and-take economy. The following proposition shows that condition D is necessary and sufficient for the First Welfare Theorem.

Proposition 3.2: A First Welfare Theorem

Let $\langle N, X, F, \Lambda \rangle$ be a convex environment.

(i) If the convex environment satisfies condition D, then for any profile of Λ-convex preferences $(\succsim^i)_{i \in N}$ any primitive equilibrium profile (a^i) of the convex economy $\langle N, X, (\succsim^i)_{i \in N}, F, \Lambda \rangle$ is weakly Pareto-optimal (there is no other feasible (b^i) such that for all i either $b^i \succ^i a^i$ or $b^i = a^i$).

(ii) If the convex environment fails condition D, then there are Λ-convex preferences $(\succsim^i)_{i \in N}$ such that the convex economy $\langle N, X, (\succsim^i)_{i \in N}, F, \Lambda \rangle$ has a primitive equilibrium profile that is not weakly Pareto-optimal.

Proof:

(i) Consider a primitive equilibrium $\langle \unrhd, (a^i) \rangle$. If (a^i) is not weakly Pareto-optimal, then there is another feasible profile (b^i) such that for all i either $b^i \succ^i a^i$ or $b^i = a^i$. Then, for all i, either $b^i \rhd a^i$ or $b^i = a^i$, contradicting condition D.

(ii) Since condition D fails, there exist two distinct feasible profiles, (a^i) and (b^i), and a primitive ordering $\unrhd$ such that for all i, $a^i \rhd b^i$ or $a^i = b^i$. Extend the convex environment to a convex economy by endowing each agent with the same Λ-convex preference relation $\unrhd$. Then, $\langle \unrhd, (b^i) \rangle$ is a primitive equilibrium that is not weakly Pareto-optimal.

Note that when condition D is satisfied, every primitive equilibrium profile is weakly Pareto-optimal, but it might be not Pareto optimal. For example, for the housing economy with two houses, two agents, preferences $a \succ^1 b$ and $a \sim^2 b$, and any set of primitive orderings, condition D holds, but $\langle a \rhd b, (b, a) \rangle$ is a primitive equilibrium with a Pareto-nonoptimal profile.

3.6   A Second Welfare Theorem

We have seen that the Second Welfare Theorem does not generally hold. Essentially, it requires the following Richness property:

Definition: Richness

The convex economy $\langle N, X, (\succsim^i), F, \Lambda \rangle$ satisfies **Richness** if the following holds: Let (a^i) be a feasible profile and $\unrhd^i$ and $\unrhd^j$ be two different primitive orderings such that (recall the notation $B(\unrhd, a^i) = \{x \mid a^i \unrhd x\}$):
(i) a^i is $\succsim^i$-maximal in $B(\unrhd^i, a^i)$ but not in $B(\unrhd^j, a^i)$; and
(ii) a^j is $\succsim^j$-maximal in $B(\unrhd^j, a^j)$ but not in $B(\unrhd^i, a^j)$.
Then, there is a pair of alternatives $(b^i, b^j) \neq (a^i, a^j)$ such that:
  (I) $(b^i, b^j, a^{-i,j}) \in F$ and (II) (b^i, b^j) Pareto-dominates (a^i, a^j)
  (That is, $b^i \succsim^i a^i$ and $b^j \succsim^j a^j$ with at least one strict preference.)

The Richness property is illustrated in Figure 3.3 using an Edgeworth box. It states that, for any feasible profile (a^i), if $\unrhd^1$ is a critical direction for agent 1 at a^1 and $\unrhd^2$ is a critical direction for agent 2 at a^2, and the directions are not identical, then there is a feasible mutually beneficial reconfiguration of their bundles (b^1, b^2), which leaves all other agents unchanged.

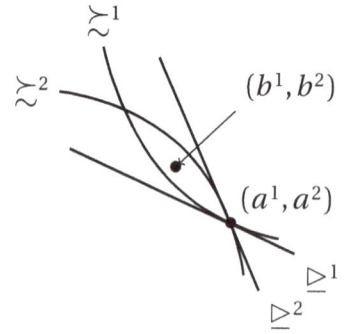

Figure 3.3 Richness

Proposition 3.3: A Second Welfare Theorem

Let $\langle N, X, (\succsim^i)_{i \in N}, F, \Lambda \rangle$ be a convex economy that satisfies Richness. Then, any Pareto-optimal profile is a primitive equilibrium profile.

Proof:

Let $(x^i)_{i \in N}$ be a Pareto-optimal profile. Let O^i be the set of all critical directions of $\succsim^i$ at x^i (that is, the set of all $\unrhd \in \Lambda$ satisfying that for any z, if $z \succ^i x^i$, then $z \rhd x^i$). By the Λ-convexity of the preferences, $O^i \neq \emptyset$.

If $\cap_i O^i$ were empty, then there would be two agents i and j such that O^i and O^j are non-nested sets. Take $\unrhd^i \in O^i \setminus O^j$ and $\unrhd^j \in O^j \setminus O^i$. The element x^i is $\succsim^i$-maximal in $B(\unrhd^i, x^i)$ but not in $B(\unrhd^j, x^i)$, and analogously for agent j. By the Richness property, there is a pair of elements (b^i, b^j) such that the modified profile obtained by replacing the pair (x^i, x^j) with (b^i, b^j) is feasible and Pareto-dominates $(x^i)_{i \in N}$, which contradicts the Pareto-optimality of (x^i). Thus, there exists $\unrhd \in \cap_i O^i$, and therefore, $\langle \unrhd, (x^i)_{i \in N} \rangle$ is a primitive equilibrium.

In Richter and Rubinstein (2015), it is shown that under the following two additional assumptions the Richness property is also necessary for the Second Welfare Theorem to hold: (i) differentiability of preferences and (ii) there are no two alternatives, x and x', such that $x \unrhd x'$ for all primitive orderings $\unrhd$.

3.7 Primitive Equilibrium – Examples

Example: The Division Economy

Let $X = \mathbb{R}^L_+$ be the set of bundles in an L-commodity world. Let $z = (z_l)$ be the vector of total endowment which has to be fully divided, that is, (x^i) is feasible if $\Sigma^n_{i=1} x^i = z$. Let Ψ_+ be the set of all positive algebraic orderings, namely all $\geq_v$ where $v \in \mathbb{R}^L_+ \backslash \{0\}$. Let the set of primitive orderings Λ be a non-empty (finite or infinite) subset of Ψ_+. All agents hold monotonic Λ-convex preference relations. Two simple cases: When Λ contains a single ordering $\geq_v$, all agents hold the same preference relation, $\succsim = \geq_v$. When $\Lambda = \{\geq_{(1,0)}, \geq_{(0,1)}\}$, every indifference curve is "right-angled".

The First Welfare Theorem holds since the economy satisfies condition D and thus, by Proposition 3.2, any primitive equilibrium profile is weakly Pareto-optimal. The Richness property used in Proposition 3.3 holds and thus any Pareto-optimal allocation is a primitive equilibrium profile. Note that this is somewhat stronger than the textbook Second Welfare Theorem which states that any Pareto-optimal allocation is an equilibrium allocation supported by *some* linear ordering while Proposition 3.3 states that the equilibrium public ordering can be drawn from Λ.

Example: The Set Allocation Economy

A non-empty finite set of distinct indivisible goods Z is to be partitioned among the agents. Unlike in the housing economy, an agent can have more than one good or none at all. Let X be the set of all subsets of Z. We will use lower-case letters for goods and the Greek symbols Θ and Φ for collections of goods. The set F contains all profiles that allocate each item in Z to exactly one agent. For every v, a positive-valued function on Z, let $\trianglerighteq_v$ be the ordering of X represented by the utility function $v(\Theta) = \Sigma_{z \in \Theta} v(z)$. That is, $v(\Theta)$ is the sum of the v-values attached to the individual items in the set Θ. Let Λ be the set of such strict orderings. It turns out (see Richter and Rubinstein (2019)) that the Λ-convex preferences are exactly all preferences that are weakly monotonic with respect to the inclusion relation. We assume that all agents' preference relations are strict and Λ-convex.

In this economy, a primitive equilibrium has the interpretation that a price is attached to *each good* and the price of a collection of goods is the sum of the prices of the goods in the collection. In contrast, a status equilibrium has the interpretation that there is a price for *each collection*.

Claim: For the set allocation economy: the set of primitive equilibrium profiles $\subseteq$ the set of Pareto-optimal profiles $\subseteq$ the set of status equilibrium profiles, and these inclusions can be strict.

Proof: To establish the first inclusion, by Proposition 3.2 it suffices to verify that condition D holds. Take a primitive ordering $\trianglerighteq_v$. For any two distinct feasible profiles, (Θ^i) and (Φ^i), it holds that $\Sigma_i v(\Theta^i) = \Sigma_i v(\Phi^i) = v(Z)$. Thus, it cannot be that $v(\Theta^i) \geq v(\Phi^i)$ for all i with at least one strict inequality.

However, there can be Pareto-optimal profiles that are not primitive equilibrium profiles. For example, let $Z = \{a, b, c, d\}$ and $n = 2$. Both agents have preferences that rank any cardinally larger set higher and are therefore, Λ-convex. To simplify notation, denote the set of goods $\{x, y\}$ as xy. Table 3.1 depicts the agents' preferences over two-element sets:

$\succsim^1$	$\succsim^2$
ac, bd	ad, bc
ab	cd
ad, bc, cd	ab, ac, bd

Table 3.1 Preferences with a Pareto-optimal profile that is not a primitive equilibrium profile (highlighted).

The profile $(x^1, x^2) = (ab, cd)$ is Pareto-optimal. However, there is no public ordering $\geq_v$ that supports this profile as a primitive equilibrium. If there were, then $ac >_v ab$ (to ensure that ab is optimal for agent 1), which implies that $v(c) > v(b)$. Similarly, we can conclude that $v(b) > v(d) > v(a) > v(c)$, a contradiction.

For the second inclusion, recall that by Proposition 3.1, any Pareto-optimal profile is a status equilibrium profile. However, there are set allocation economies with status equilibrium profiles that are not Pareto-optimal. For example, suppose that $Z = \{a, b, c, d\}$, $n = 2$, and both agents have the same Λ-convex preferences $\succsim^*$ satisfying that the sets ac and bd are $\succsim^*$-superior to ab and cd. Then, $\langle P = \succsim^*, (ab, cd) \rangle$ is a status equilibrium that is not Pareto-optimal. ∎

This example demonstrates a stark contrast between equilibria with item-pricing (where the price of a bundle is the sum of the individual items' prices) and those with bundle-pricing (where a price is attached to each bundle). The following table summarizes the above claim:

	Item-pricing equilibria	Bundle-pricing equilibria
First Welfare Theorem	✓	X
Second Welfare Theorem	X	✓

Table 3.2 Depiction of the Claim

3.8 Initial Status Equilibrium

In this section, we extend the definition of a status equilibrium to cover extended economies. To remind the reader, an extended economy is an economy with the specification of an additional feasible profile $(e^i)_{i \in N}$ interpreted as an "initial profile". It specifies an alternative for each agent which he has the absolute right to choose, independently of other agents' choices and of the equilibrium parameters. When the alternatives are assets, the initial profile can be thought of as specifying initial ownership.

> ### Definition: Initial Status Equilibrium
>
> Given an extended economy $\langle N, X, (\succsim^i)_{i \in N}, F, (e^i)_{i \in N} \rangle$:
>
> An **initial status equilibrium** is a pair $\langle P, (x^i)_{i \in N} \rangle$ where P is an ordering on X and (x^i) is a feasible profile such that every agent i's assigned alternative x^i is $\succsim^i$-optimal in his "budget set" $B(P, e^i) = \{x \in X \mid e^i P x\}$.

In an initial status equilibrium, an agent's choice set consists of all alternatives that are weakly P-inferior to his *initial alternative*. In contrast, in a status equilibrium, an agent's choice set consists of all alternatives that are weakly P-inferior to his *equilibrium alternative*.

Two comments:

(i) If x^i is $\succsim^i$-maximal in $B(P, e^i)$, then x^i is also $\succsim^i$-maximal in $B(P, x^i)$. Thus, any initial status equilibrium of an extended economy is also a status equilibrium of the underlying economy.

(ii) If $\langle P, (x^i) \rangle$ is a status equilibrium, then for every strict ordering P' which is a tiebreaking of P, the pair $\langle P', (x^i) \rangle$ is also a status equilibrium. This is not the case for an initial status equilibrium: Consider the extended housing economy with two houses a and b, two agents, initial profile $(e^1, e^2) = (a, b)$, and preference relations $b \succ^1 a$ and $a \succ^2 b$. The public ordering that equally ranks a and b and the profile (b, a) constitute an initial status equilibrium for the extended economy. However, breaking this indifference will invalidate the equilibrium since one of the two agents will not be able to "afford" the other house.

Even though a status equilibrium exists when a Pareto-optimal profile does (Proposition 3.1), the following example demonstrates that the existence of an initial status equilibrium is not guaranteed even for finite extended economies.

Example: An Extended Jobs Economy

Consider the jobs economy of Section 3.2 with 3 agents, two jobs a and b, and capacities $n_a = 2$ and $n_b = 1$. Assume that agents 1 and 2 prefer b and agent 3 prefers a.

There are two Pareto-optimal profiles (b, a, a) and (a, b, a), both of which are status equilibrium profiles (with the public ordering bPa). If either of those profiles is the initial profile, then it is also an initial status equilibrium profile.

However, if the initial profile is (a, a, b), where each agent starts with the alternative he dislikes, then an initial status equilibrium does not exist. To see why, note that an equilibrium public ordering cannot rank a weakly above b, because then agents 1 and 2 would both choose b, violating feasibility. Nor can it be that b is ranked strictly above a, because then all three agents would choose a, again violating feasibility. The "problem" is that the initial status equilibrium concept does not allow for the exchange of a and b between 1 and 3 (or between 2 and 3) due to the equilibrium concept's inability in allowing different budget sets for two agents with the same initial alternative.

The reader may wonder why no equilibrium exists in this extended economy whereas an equilibrium does exist in the standard competitive market model. The reason is that, in the standard competitive market model there is also money in the economy and a monetary amount can be attached to the transaction of exchanging a for b so that at least one of the two agents who prefer b to a would be indifferent between conducting the transaction or refraining from it. Then, the public ordering in the standard market is not merely ordinal but cardinal, indicating the monetary amount required to exchange a lower-ranked good for a higher-ranked one.

Thus, the existence of an initial status equilibrium is not guaranteed when the initial profile assigns identical elements to different agents. However, whenever every agent has a distinct initial alternative, the following proposition establishes the existence of an initial status equilibrium. Furthermore, it shows that if in addition there is a strict partial ordering R such that all individual preferences are R-monotonic (that is, if aRb then $a \succ^i b$ for all i), then there is an R-monotonic equilibrium public ordering. Taking R to be the empty binary relation gives the baseline result of Shapley and Scarf (1974) (presented in Section 1.3).

Proposition 3.4: Existence of an Initial Status Equilibrium

Any extended economy $\langle N, X, (\succsim^i)_{i \in N}, F, (e^i)_{i \in N} \rangle$ where all initial alternatives are distinct has an initial status equilibrium. If, in addition, all preference relations are R-monotonic with respect to a strict partial ordering R, then the public ordering can be taken to be R-monotonic as well.

Proof:

Let Y be the set of alternatives in the initial profile (e^i). For any $Z \subseteq Y$, define $M(Z) = \{i \mid e^i = z \text{ for some } z \in Z\}$ to be the set of agents initially assigned to alternatives in Z. Following the construction in Proposition 1.5, select a sequence of top trading cycles, $B^1, \ldots, B^T$. Define a partial ordering P on Y by aPb if $a \in B^t$, $b \in B^s$, and $t \leq s$ (all elements in the same B^t are P-indifferent). We need to extend P to all of X. Partition $X \backslash Y$ into sets $A^1, \ldots, A^{T+1}$ as follows: For any $x \in X \backslash Y$, let $x \in A^t$ where t is the smallest index such that there is an agent $i \in M(B^t)$ who strictly prefers x over all elements in B^t. If there is no such t, then let $x \in A^{T+1}$. Place the elements in any A^t below B^{t-1} and above B^t. Define P on A^t as any arbitrary expansion of R. To see that P expands R everywhere, consider a and b such that aRb (and thus, all agents prefer a to b).

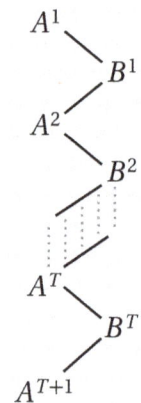

Figure 3.4
The Construction

- If $b \in Y$, then $b \in B^t$ for some t. If $a \in Y$, then it must belong to an earlier trading cycle because no agent would top-rank b when a is present, and thus, aPb. If $a \notin Y$, then the agent who top-ranks $b \in B^t$ prefers a to all elements of B^t. Therefore, $a \in A^s$ with $s \leq t$, thus, aPb.

- If $b \in A^t$ for some $t \leq T$, then for some $i \in M(B^t)$ it holds that $b \succ^i y$ for all $y \in B^t$. Thus, i also prefers a over all $y \in B^t$. If $a \in Y$, then a belongs to a previous trading cycle and if $a \notin Y$, then it belongs to A^s with $s \leq t$. In either case aPb (for the case that $a, b \in A^t$, recall that P expands R on A^t).

- If $b \in A^{T+1}$ and $a \notin A^{T+1}$, then aPb and if $a \in A^{T+1}$, then aPb because P expands R on A^{T+1}.

The profile (y^i), which assigns to each agent $i \in M(B^t)$ the element y^i that e^i points to in the top trading cycle B^t, together with P, constitutes an initial status equilibrium: First, (y^i) is feasible since it is a permutation of the initial profile. Second, for every i, e^iPy^i because y^i and e^i are in the same cycle. Third, suppose that $z \succ^i y^i$ for some agent i. Then, if $z \in Y$, it belongs to an earlier cycle. If $z \notin Y$, then i prefers z to all elements of B^t, and so $z \in A^s$ for $s \leq t$. In either event, zPy^i.

Example: The Extended Give-and-Take Economy

Extend the give-and-take economy by adding an initial profile $(e^i)_{i \in N}$ that is feasible, $\Sigma e^i = 0$. Each agent i for whom $e^i > 0$ has the right to take e^i from the public fund, while each agent i for whom $e^i < 0$ has the right to contribute $-e^i$. Remember that every agent i has continuous and strictly convex (and thus single-peaked) preferences with a peak at $peak^i$. As before, we focus on the case where $\Sigma peak^i > 0$. Here, we adopt the interpretation that aPb means that b is more socially beneficial than a. Each agent chooses how much to give or take from the alternatives that are more socially beneficial than his initial assignment.

The existence of an initial status equilibrium for this extended economy is guaranteed by Proposition 3.4 only for the case that all e^i are distinct. Here, we construct a simple initial status equilibrium with an attractive structure which also demonstrates existence even when the e^i are not distinct.

Let P_z be the ordering that places all alternatives between -1 and z equally at the bottom and is strictly increasing from z to 1. Every agent i faces the interval budget set $[-1, \max\{z, e^i\}]$ and so has a unique optimal choice which is continuous in z, weakly increasing, and strictly increasing for $z \in [e^i, peak^i]$ (in the case that $e^i < peak^i$). Given the total indifference ordering P_1, every agent would choose $peak^i$, and the sum of their chosen actions would be $\Sigma_i peak^i > 0$. Given the strictly increasing ordering P_{-1}, every agent i chooses an alternative $x^i \leq e^i$ and the sum of the chosen alternatives is non-positive since $\Sigma_i x^i \leq \Sigma_i e^i = 0$. Thus, by the continuity of the agents' choices in z, there is a $z^* \in [-1, 1]$ for which the sum of the chosen elements is 0. The ordering P_{z^*} together with the profile of optimal choices from the corresponding budget sets is an initial status equilibrium.

4 Biased Preferences Equilibrium

In any economy, the core tension is between agents' wants and societal feasibility, and an equilibrium notion finds a balance between them. In Chapters 2 and 3, we investigated equilibrium notions that invoke various social mechanisms to achieve that balance: norms emerge that affect agents' opportunity sets such that if every agent optimizes his preference relation, then the profile of optimal choices is feasible.

This chapter takes a different approach. We follow Rubinstein and Wolinksy (2022) who propose a solution concept which captures a different social mechanism that can resolve the fundamental conflict between wants and feasibility: *agents' preference relations are systematically biased.* The bias does not affect the agents' opportunity sets but, rather, their preferences, which are systematically biased in such a way that the profile of agents' *biased optimal choices* is feasible.

Recall Aesop's classic fable (translation from Gibbs (2002)):

> Driven by hunger, a fox tried to reach some grapes hanging high
> on the vine but was unable to, although he leaped with all his
> strength. As he went away, the fox remarked "Oh, you aren't even
> ripe yet! I don't need any sour grapes."

In this fable, there is one agent, the Fox, and two alternatives, "picking the grapes" and "not picking the grapes". The economic problem is that the Fox initially prefers the former alternative but only the latter alternative is feasible. The conflict in the fable is resolved not by restricting the Fox's opportunities but, rather, by biasing his preferences so that he now prefers not to pick the grapes (which in his mind are turned to "sour grapes").

     https://doi.org/10.11647/OBP.0404.04

Preference biases are not just a matter for fables. Introspection tells us that feasibility often influences our preferences in everyday life. We often assign greater value to what we can obtain (such as being an economist) and less to what we cannot (such as being a mathematician). However, we do not deny that there are also circumstances where the opposite is true, and the more unobtainable something is the more desirable it becomes.

The Fox biased his preferences, and harmony was achieved. Similarly, we envision biases as a mechanism for bringing harmony to a multi-agent economy. These biases, like prices, will be systematic and apply uniformly to all agents. Every agent's final preferences are determined by both the commonly shared bias and his initial preferences. Thus, in contrast to a competitive equilibrium where prices affect choice sets and preferences are fixed, in a biased preferences equilibrium biases affect preferences and choice sets are fixed. This illustrates the dual roles played by prices and preferences in standard economic settings.

Note the difference between this chapter's approach and the one taken by other economic models. In some of those models, the change in preferences is a side effect of an agent's action (for example, smoking may influence the desire to smoke in the future, as modelled by Becker and Murphy (1988)). In others, the change in preferences is the outcome of a deliberate action by an interested party (for example, advertisers seek to influence customers' preferences to their own advantage, as modelled by Bagwell (2007)). By contrast, this chapter models social situations in which preferences invisibly respond to feasibility pressures, just as price adjustments achieve harmony in a competitive market.

4.1   The Economy and the Equilibrium Concept

In this chapter, the notion of an economy is modified to accommodate modelling systematic preference biases.

Definition: An Economy

An **economy** is a tuple $\langle N, (X^i)_{i \in N}, K, ((u^i_k)_{k \in K})_{i \in N}, F \rangle$ where:

- For each agent i, X^i is his *fixed* personal choice set.

- The set K is a set of **considerations** common to all agents.

- For each agent i, $(u^i_k)_{k \in K}$ is a tuple of **consideration functions** over X^i such that i's utility function over X^i is $\Sigma_k u^i_k(x)$.

- The set of feasible profiles, F, is a subset of $\Pi_{i \in N} X^i$.

This definition modifies our notion of an economy in two ways. First, and less importantly, different agents can have different choice sets. This allows for modelling a variety of settings. For example, an exchange economy with a set of goods K, a fixed price vector p, and initial endowment profile (e^i) can be modelled by setting $X^i = \{x \in \mathbb{R}^K_+ \mid p \cdot x = p \cdot e^i\}$ and $F = \{(x^i) \mid \Sigma x^i = \Sigma e^i\}$. Another example is a two-sided matching market with two equally-sized populations A and B. This can be modelled by setting $X^i = B$ for any $i \in A$ and $X^j = A$ for any $j \in B$, while F is the set of all profiles (x^i) for which for every i, j, $x^i = j$ implies $x^j = i$.

The second and more important modification of the original definition of an economy is the use of a different notion of preferences. Rather than specifying an ordinal preference relation over the set of alternatives, we use the following type of utility function that enables us to model systematic biases. All agents share the same set of considerations K. Each agent i is characterized not by an ordinal preference relation, but by a vector of consideration functions $u^i = (u^i_k)_{k \in K}$ where $u^i_k(x)$ represents the impact of consideration k on his overall evaluation of the alternative x. The consideration functions are not constant and, where applicable, are differentiable. Agent i's overall utility from an alternative x is the sum of the utilities obtained from those considerations, i.e. $\Sigma_{k \in K} u^i_k(x)$.

A preference bias is modelled as a systematic and uniform change in the weights placed on the considerations. Let $\Lambda = \mathbb{R}^K_{++}$ be the set of *biases*. A bias

$\lambda = (\lambda_k)_{k \in K}$ transforms *every* vector of consideration functions $u = (u_k)_{k \in K}$ into the vector of biased consideration functions $T(u, \lambda) = (\lambda_k u_k)_{k \in K}$. That is, if an agent i enters the model with the vector of consideration functions (u_k^i) and the bias vector is (λ_k), then the agent behaves as if his vector of consideration functions is $(\lambda_k u_k^i)$ and chooses from X^i by maximizing $\sum_{k \in K} \lambda_k u_k^i(x)$. The preferences are unbiased when $\lambda = (c, \ldots, c)$ because (u_k^i) and $(c u_k^i)$ induce the same preferences. Thus, any bias can be normalized to sum to 1 and therefore, can be naturally interpreted as a vector of weights on the different considerations.

The specification of K consideration functions is important beyond inducing an agent's preference relation. Two vectors of consideration functions, $u = (u_k)$ and $v = (v_k)$, can induce the *same* preference relation, and yet their biased preferences, $T(u, \lambda)$ and $T(v, \lambda)$, may induce *different* preference relations, as shown in the following example:

Let $K = \{1, 2\}$, $X^1 = X^2 = \{0, 1\} \times \{0, 1\}$ (the four corners of the unit square), $u_1(x) = x_1$, $u_2(x) = 4x_2$, and $v_1(x) = x_1$, $v_2(x) = 2x_2$. Both (u_k) and (v_k) induce the same preferences $(1, 1) \succ (0, 1) \succ (1, 0) \succ (0, 0)$, but when the bias vector is $\lambda = (3, 1)$, the preferences induced by $T((u_k), \lambda)$ are unchanged while the preferences induced by $T((v_k), \lambda)$ become $(1, 1) \succ (1, 0) \succ (0, 1) \succ (0, 0)$.

On the other hand, when the set of alternatives X is the positive orthant of an Euclidean space, any two additively separable, monotonic, and differentiable utility functions that represent the same preferences on X are transformed by the bias map T into the same biased preferences.

Claim: Preference Preservation in Euclidean Spaces

Let $X = \mathbb{R}_+^{|K|}$ be the common set of alternatives. Let $u = (u_k)_{k \in K}$ and $v = (v_k)_{k \in K}$ be vectors of consideration functions, so that both u_k and v_k depend only on x_k and are differentiable with strictly positive derivatives. If u and v induce identical preference relations, then for any λ, the biased preferences induced by $T(u, \lambda)$ and $T(v, \lambda)$ are identical.

Proof:

The case $K = \{1\}$ is vacuous since the only admissible preference relation is the increasing ordering on $\mathbb{R}_+$.

Let $|K| \geq 2$. Since u and v represent the same preferences, then at any $x \in X$ the gradient of the utility function $V(x) = \Sigma v_k(x_k)$ is a rescaling of the gradient of $U(x) = \Sigma u_k(x_k)$. That is, for every x, there is a strictly positive scalar $\mu(x) > 0$ such that $\nabla V(x) = \mu(x)\nabla U(x)$. It suffices to show that $\mu(x)$ is a constant μ since then $v'_k(x_k) = \mu u'_k(x_k)$ for all k and x_k, and therefore $v_k(x_k) = \mu u_k(x_k) + c_k$ for some c_k. Thus, $\Sigma \lambda_k v_k(x_k) = \Sigma \lambda_k (\mu u_k(x_k) + c_k) = \mu \Sigma \lambda_k u_k(x_k) + \Sigma \lambda_k c_k$ and therefore, the biased utility functions are an affine transformation of each other and, as such, represent the same preferences over X.

To show that $\mu(x)$ is a constant, notice that if two bundles x and y share a coordinate $x_k = y_k$, then $\mu(x) = \mu(y)$ since $v'_k(x_k) = \mu(x)u'_k(x_k)$ and $v'_k(y_k) = \mu(y)u'_k(y_k)$. If they do not share a coordinate, then let z be a bundle such that $z_1 = x_1$ and $z_2 = y_2$. Since z shares a coordinate with each of them, it must be that $\mu(x) = \mu(z) = \mu(y)$.

Generalizing the bias concept. The bias notion has been formalized for preference relations induced from an additively separable representation $\Sigma_k u_k(x)$. In particular, when X is a subset of a Euclidean space and u_k is a function only of x_k, a bias vector (λ_k) multiplies the subjective tradeoff between any two goods k and l by λ_k/λ_l.

This suggests a generalization of the bias concept to more general preference relations where the biased preference tradeoffs are obtained by systematically multiplying the agent's unbiased tradeoffs. This generalization can be shown when $K = 2$ and preferences are differentiable. More precisely, for any preference relation $\succsim$, denote the marginal rate of substitution between k and l at a bundle x by $MRS_{k,l}(x, \succsim)$. For every vector of biases (λ_1, λ_2), there is another preference relation $\succsim'$ for which $MRS_{1,2}(x, \succsim') = \frac{\lambda_1}{\lambda_2}MRS_{1,2}(x, \succsim)$ for every bundle x. However, this is not always possible when $K > 2$:

Example: The Difficulty in Extending the Bias Notion

Let $K = \{1,2,3\}$ and $\succsim$ be represented by u where $u(x_1, x_2, 0) = 2x_1$ and $u(x_1, x_2, 1) = x_1 + x_2$. Let the bias vector be $\lambda = (\lambda_k) = (1,2,1)$. Suppose that there are biased preferences $\succsim^\lambda$ such that for any two goods k and l, $MRS_{k,l}(x, \succsim^\lambda) = \frac{\lambda_k}{\lambda_l} MRS_{k,l}(x, \succsim)$ at every alternative x. Then:

(i) The $MRS_{1,2}$ is unchanged (and remains ∞) at every $(x_1, x_2, 0)$.

(ii) The $MRS_{1,2}$ is changed from 1 to 1/2 at every $(x_1, x_2, 1)$.

(iii) The $MRS_{1,3}$ is unchanged at any alternative.

By (i) and (iii), it holds that $(3,5,1) \sim^\lambda (4,5,0) \sim^\lambda (4,6,0) \sim^\lambda (2,6,1)$ because $u(3,5,1) = u(4,5,0) = u(4,6,0) = u(2,6,1)$. But then, $(3,5,1) \sim^\lambda (2,6,1)$, contradicting (ii). Thus, there is no preference relation $\succsim^\lambda$ for which all biased marginal rates of substitution are λ-scaled versions of the original.

We now define the solution concept. As explained above, harmony will be achieved by a uniform social shift of the weights placed on the consideration functions. An equilibrium consists of a profile (x^i) of alternatives and a bias λ such that: (i) for every agent i, the alternative x^i is optimal in X^i according to his biased preferences; and (ii) the profile is feasible.

Definition: Biased Preferences Equilibrium

A *biased preferences equilibrium* is a tuple $\langle \lambda, (x^i) \rangle$ where $\lambda \in \Lambda$ and (x^i) is a profile of choices, such that:

(i) For every agent i, the alternative x^i is optimal in X^i according to the preferences induced by $T(u^i, \lambda)$.

(ii) The profile (x^i) is in F.

We will refer to a profile of alternatives that is Pareto-optimal according to the agents' initial preferences as *pre-Pareto optimal*. Obviously, since agents choose optimally given their biased preferences, a profile of biased preferences equilibrium·choices is always ex-post Pareto optimal.

Example: The Kosher Economy

We return to the "kosher" economy with two pies of size 1. The feasibility constraint stipulates that the total consumption of neither pie exceeds 1. The consumption sets $X^i = \{(a_1, 0) \mid 0 \leq a_1 \leq 1\} \cup \{(0, a_2) \mid 0 \leq a_2 \leq 1\}$ are the same for all agents. Each agent i has two continuous and concave consideration functions, $v_1^i(x_1)$ and $v_2^i(x_2)$, where x_k is the amount consumed of pie k. Denote v_k^i's peak by $peak_k^i$. Thus, each agent i will choose either $peak_1^i$ of pie 1 or $peak_2^i$ of pie 2. Given a bias λ, he will choose pie k only if $\lambda_k v_k^i(peak_k^i) \geq \lambda_l v_l^i(peak_l^i)$ where l is the other pie.

Let $\alpha^i = v_1^i(peak_1^i)/v_2^i(peak_2^i)$ and assume that all α^i are distinct. Without loss of generality, suppose that $\alpha^1 > \alpha^2 > \cdots > \alpha^n$. Given a bias vector λ, denote $\mu = \lambda_2/\lambda_1$. An agent i will choose $peak_1^i$ of pie 1 if $\alpha^i > \mu$, $peak_2^i$ of pie 2 if $\alpha^i < \mu$, and will be indifferent between them if $\alpha^i = \mu$.

In the following economy, there is a unique biased preferences equilibrium profile, but it is not pre-Pareto optimal. Agents $1, \ldots, 4$ initially prefer to consume from the first pie (since their α^i are above 1), while agent 5 initially prefers to consume from the second ($\alpha^5 < 1$).

Agent	α^i	$peak_1^i$	$peak_2^i$
1	5	0.3	0.2
2	4	0.6	0.2
3	3	0.5	0.1
4	2	0.1	0.7
5	1/3	0.3	0.1

Table 4.1 An equilibrium in the Kosher economy

The biased preferences equilibrium profile is unique: agents 1 and 2 choose their peaks from the first pie while the others choose their peaks from the second pie. It is supported by any bias for which $3 \leq \mu \leq 4$. This is not a pre-Pareto optimal profile since there is a surplus of 0.1 of the first pie, and agent 4 initially prefers 0.1 of pie 1 to 0.7 of the second pie.

Giving him the leftovers from the first pie is a Pareto improvement that is impossible in the biased preferences equilibrium because blocking agent 3 from consuming from the first pie forces the bias to be such that agent 4 is also biased towards consuming a slice of the second pie.

Of course, an equilibrium may not exist. For example, if the above table is modified so that $peak_2^3 = 0.4$ (instead of 0.1), then no biased preferences equilibrium exists.

In the rest of the chapter, we analyze the biased preferences equilibrium for several examples: the give-and-take economy, the exchange economy with fixed prices, and a few housing-type economies.

4.2   The Give-and-Take Economy

We return to an old friend: the give-and-take economy. Recall that, in this economy, each agent decides how much to contribute to or withdraw from a social fund, and feasibility requires that the total contributions equal the total withdrawals. All agents face the same choice set $[-1, 1]$, where, as usual, a positive number represents the amount taken from (and a negative number the amount given to) the social fund. To fit it into the current framework, let the two considerations be g (giving) and t (taking). The consideration g is generous (people like to give), while the consideration t is selfish (people like to take). Initially, an agent i's choice balances between these two considerations by choosing the maximizer of $u_g^i(x) + u_t^i(x)$, where u_g^i is a strictly decreasing function and u_t^i is a strictly increasing function, both of which are strictly concave. Denote by $peak^i$ the unique maximizer of $u_g^i(x) + u_t^i(x)$, which is agent i's most-preferred choice in $[-1, 1]$, and assume that it is interior.

Any bias λ pushes all agents' preferences in the same direction by systematically altering the tradeoff between generosity and selfishness. Denote $\mu = \lambda_t / \lambda_g$. A μ above 1 biases the agents' preferences towards selfishness, while a μ below 1 biases the agents' preferences towards generosity.

Under the above assumptions, there is a unique equilibrium profile, and it is pre-Pareto optimal:

Proposition 4.1: Uniqueness and Pre-Pareto Optimality

(i) The give-and-take economy has a unique biased preferences equilibrium (up to a rescaling of the bias vector).

(ii) The equilibrium profile is pre-Pareto optimal.

Proof:

(i) Given the bias $(1, \mu)$, each agent i optimizes $u_g^i(x) + \mu \cdot u_t^i(x)$ and has a unique optimal choice denoted by $x^i(\mu)$. Since all of the x^i functions are increasing and continuous, so is the net overall "demand" from the social fund, $\Sigma_i x^i(\mu)$. This sum is positive when μ is sufficiently large and negative when μ is sufficiently small. Therefore, there is a μ^* for which the sum is zero, and $\langle (1, \mu^*), (x^i(\mu^*)) \rangle$ is a biased preferences equilibrium. The parameter μ^* is unique since $x^i(\mu)$ is strictly increasing when $-1 < x^i(\mu) < 1$, and it must be that $x^i(\mu^*)$ is interior for some i (if $\mu \geq 1$, then for every i, $x^i(\mu^*) \geq peak^i > -1$ and it cannot be that for every i, $x^i(\mu^*) = 1$; the case $\mu \leq 1$ is analogous).

(ii) If $\mu^* = 1$, then every agent's equilibrium choice is his unbiased first-best. If $\mu^* > 1$, then every agent i chooses $x^i(\mu^*) \geq peak^i$, and any ex-ante Pareto improvement (y^i) must satisfy $y^i \leq x^i(\mu^*)$ with at least one strict inequality, but that contradicts feasibility since $0 = \Sigma x^i(\mu^*) > \Sigma y^i$. Thus, the equilibrium profile is pre-Pareto optimal. The case $\mu^* < 1$ is analogous.

Note that in the biased preferences equilibrium, balancing the social fund is a shared responsibility of all agents: when the sum of the agents' peaks is positive (i.e. there is an overall preference for taking), the equilibrium bias ($\mu^* < 1$) overweighs generosity and *every* agent chooses a point below his peak. This is essentially true for primitive equilibria (in every equilibrium profile all agents are assigned to alternatives weakly below their peaks). In contrast, in a Y-equilibrium, there is a uniform cap on withdrawals and only the greediest agents are impacted, and in a jungle equilibrium, only the weakest agents are restricted.

4.3   The Fixed-Prices Exchange Economy

The next example is related to the literature on economies with fixed prices (see Benassy (1986) and the references therein). Let $X = \mathbb{R}^K_{++}$ be the set of bundles in a world with a set of goods K. Every agent i has an initial endowment $e^i \in X$, and exchange takes place according to a fixed price vector $p = (p_k)$. Accordingly, $X^i = \{x \in X \mid p \cdot x = p \cdot e^i\}$, and the set of feasible profiles is $F = \{(x^i) \in \Pi_i X^i \mid \Sigma_i x^i = \Sigma_i e^i\}$. All agents share the same considerations, one for each good. Each consideration function $u^i_k(x)$ is a function of only x_k, which is assumed to be increasing, twice-differentiable, and strictly concave.

In economies with fixed prices, rationing is typically the mechanism used to achieve harmony. That is, upper bounds are established on the consumable quantity of each good. In contrast, in a biased preferences equilibrium, economic harmony is achieved by means of a systematic adjustment of preferences.

> ### Proposition 4.2: Biased Preferences Equilibria in Exchange Economies with Fixed Prices
>
> In any exchange economy with fixed prices:
> (i) A biased preferences equilibrium exists.
> (ii) All biased preferences equilibrium outcomes are pre-Pareto optimal.

> ### Proof:
>
> (i) To illustrate, consider the two-good two-agent case, which can be depicted using an Edgeworth Box (see Figure 4.1). Assume that agents do not like consuming on the boundary, i.e. the derivative of every

consideration function u_k^i at 0 is infinity. Let (x^1, x^2) be a Pareto-optimal feasible allocation of $e^1 + e^2$, which always exists. Then, at (x^1, x^2), both agents have the same marginal rate of substitution μ. If $\mu = p_1/p_2$, then no bias is needed, that is, $\langle \lambda = (1, 1), (x^i) \rangle$ is a biased preferences equilibrium. If $\mu \neq p_1/p_2$, then the bias $\lambda = (p_1, p_2\mu)$ modifies both preferences so that the $MRS_{1,2}$ of the biased preferences of each i at x^i is $\mu\lambda_1/\lambda_2 = p_1/p_2$. Thus, $\langle \lambda, (x^i) \rangle$ is a biased preferences equilibrium.

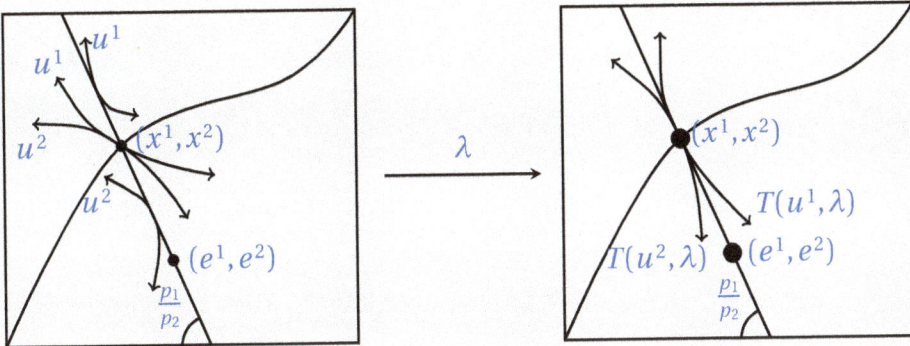

Figure 4.1 Equilibrium in an Edgeworth Box

For the case of more than two goods and any number of agents, Keiding (1981) (following Balasko (1979)) showed that there is a vector $q = (q_k)$ and an allocation (x^i) such that $p \cdot x^i = p \cdot e^i$ for all i, and if $y^i \succ^i x^i$, then $q \cdot y^i > q \cdot x^i$. Therefore, for every agent i, any good l that he consumes and any other good k, it holds that $MRS_{k,l}$ at x^i is bounded from above by q_k/q_l. Consequently, by setting $\lambda = (p_k/q_k)_{k \in K}$, it holds that for agent i's biased preferences and any good l that he consumes, the $MRS_{k,l}$ at x^i is bounded from above by $p_k/p_l = \lambda_k q_k/\lambda_l q_l$ (the bound is an equality if $x_k^i > 0$). Therefore, for every agent i, given the price vector p and the initial bundle e^i, the bundle x^i is optimal for i's biased preferences. Thus, $\langle \lambda, (x^i) \rangle$ is a biased preferences equilibrium.

(ii) Let $\langle \lambda, (x^i) \rangle$ be a biased preferences equilibrium. Then, for each agent i and any good l that he consumes, the $MRS_{k,l}$ of the biased preferences $T(\lambda, u^i)$ at x^i is bounded from above by p_k/p_l. Therefore, the $MRS_{k,l}$ of his initial preferences at x^i is bounded from above by $\frac{p_k/\lambda_k}{p_l/\lambda_l}$. Thus, (x^i) is a Walrasian equilibrium outcome in the unbiased economy with price vector (p_k/λ_k) and initial endowment (x^i). Therefore, by the standard First Welfare Theorem, (x^i) is pre-Pareto optimal.

We now consider an example with two goods and linear preferences where the biased preferences equilibrium can easily be calculated.

Example: Linear Preferences

Suppose that there are two agents, two goods, and that for every agent i, the two consideration functions are linear, that is, $u_1^i(x_1) = x_1$ and $u_2^i(x_2) = \alpha^i x_2$ where every α^i is a positive number. Consider the configuration depicted in Figure 4.2:

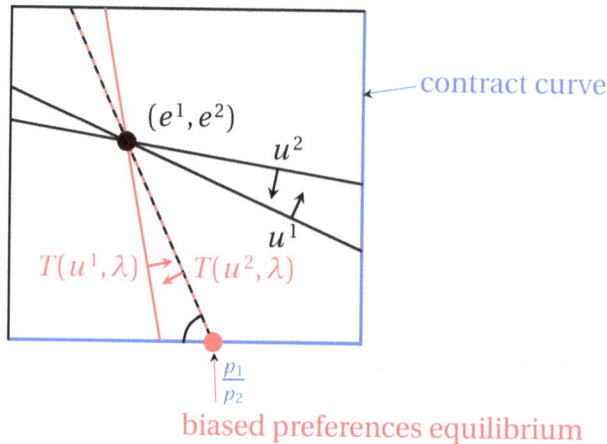

Figure 4.2 Biased linear preferences in an Edgeworth Box (dashed line = the budget lines; black solid lines = initial preferences; red solid lines = biased preferences; blue line = the contract curve for the initial preferences)

In this example (other configurations can be analyzed similarly):

(i) Agent 2 likes good 2 more than agent 1 does, that is, $\alpha^2 > \alpha^1$.

(ii) The ratio p_1/p_2 is greater than both agents' (constant) personal marginal rates of substitution, that is, $p_1/p_2 > 1/\alpha^1 > 1/\alpha^2$.

(iii) In any feasible allocation, both agents must consume positive amounts of good 1.

The economy is not in harmony because, given (ii), both agents wish to purchase only good 2.

In any biased preferences equilibrium, there is an agent i who consumes good 2, and by (iii), he also consumes good 1. By the linearity of the preferences, agent i must be indifferent between all alternatives in X^i, that is, $p_1/p_2 = \lambda_1/(\alpha^i \lambda_2)$. If $i = 1$, then by (i), agent 2 does not consume good 1, violating (iii). Thus, it must be that $i = 2$, and the bias satisfies $p_1/p_2 = \lambda_1/(\alpha^2 \lambda_2)$.

Such a bias is part of the equilibrium depicted in Figure 4.2, where agent 1 consumes only good 1, and agent 2 (who is indifferent between all bundles in his budget set) consumes all of good 2 and the remainder of good 1. It follows that this is the unique biased preferences equilibrium.

Failure of Individual Rationality: An interesting feature of a biased preferences equilibrium is that, even though it is pre-Pareto optimal, "Individual Rationality" can fail: in an equilibrium, an agent might choose a bundle that is inferior to his endowment bundle when judged by his initial preferences, as in the previous example. By his original preferences, agent 1 is worse off in the equilibrium than he was with his initial endowment, since he trades some of his good 2 endowment for good 1, but ex-ante he would prefer to do the opposite.

Example: Non-Convex Preferences

In the standard exchange economy with non-convex preferences, a competitive equilibrium may not exist: there may be no price vector for which the sum of the demands equals the total bundle. Nevertheless, there may be a price vector for which a biased preferences equilibrium exists. Thus, prices and biased preferences together may achieve harmony when the standard competitive equilibrium tools fail to do so.

To illustrate, consider the division economy where both agents have the non-convex preferences represented by $(x_1)^2 + 2(x_2)^2$ and the initial endowments are $e^1 = (1,1)$ and $e^2 = (2,2)$. There is no standard competitive equilibrium. Given any price vector, each agent will consume only one of the two goods, and since the agents have the same preferences, any equilibrium price vector must make each agent indifferent between the two goods, i.e. $p = (1, \sqrt{2})$. But, then agent 2 will demand more than 3 units of one of the goods.

In contrast, a biased preferences equilibrium exists. Let $p = (2,1)$ and $\lambda = (8,1)$. Each agent's biased utility function is $4(x_1)^2 + (x_2)^2$. Agent 1's optimal bundles are $(1.5,0)$ and $(0,3)$, and agent 2's optimal bundles are $(3,0)$ and $(0,6)$. Thus, the bias λ, together with the allocation $x^1 = (0,3)$ and $x^2 = (3,0)$, is a biased preferences equilibrium in the exchange economy with fixed prices p.

Note that agent 1 is initially poorer than agent 2, but in the equilibrium, agent 1 is actually better off according to the initial preferences!

4.4   Housing-Type Economies

We return to the classic housing economy of Shapley and Scarf (1974), in which there is a set N of agents and an equally-sized set H of houses. Each agent i chooses a single house, that is, $X^i = H$. Let $v^i(h) > 0$ be agent i's valuation of house h. The model can be enriched to fit our framework by taking the set of considerations to be H and setting $u_h^i(x^i) = v^i(h)$ if $x^i = h$ and 0 otherwise. Given a bias vector (λ_h), an agent i derives utility $\lambda_h v^i(h)$ from house h.

Example:

The following table presents the consideration function values in a housing economy with two agents.

	h_1	h_2
$v^1(h)$	4	3
$v^2(h)$	3	1

Table 4.2 House utilities

Both agents initially prefer house h_1. To achieve harmony, the bias must boost h_2 so that one agent will choose it, but not to the extent that both will. For example, a biased preferences equilibrium is obtained by the bias $(1,2)$, which results in agent 1 choosing h_2 and agent 2 choosing h_1. Of course, other biases are possible but, in all biased preferences equilibria, agent 1 gets h_2 and agent 2 gets h_1. Note that, in the biased preferences equilibrium profile, the product of the ex-ante values $(3 \cdot 3 = 9)$ is larger than that in the other assignment $(4 \cdot 1 = 4)$. We will see below that this is not a coincidence.

We say that a feasible profile (x^i) is *Nash maximal* if it maximizes $\Pi_{i \in N} v^i(x^i)$ over all feasible profiles. We now show that the set of biased preferences equilibrium profiles is precisely the set of Nash-maximal profiles and thus, any biased preferences equilibrium profile is pre-Pareto optimal. The proof is a direct application of Shapley and Shubik (1971) (see also Gale (1984) for a proof using the KKM Lemma).

Proposition 4.3: Biased Preferences Equilibrium = Nash Maximality

In the housing economy, the set of biased preferences equilibrium profiles is the set of Nash-maximal profiles.

Proof:

Let $(h^i)_{i \in N}$ be a Nash-maximal profile, that is, it maximizes $\Sigma_{i \in N} \ln(v^i(x^i))$ over all feasible assignments. By Shapley and Shubik (1971), there exists a price vector (p_h) so that for each agent i, the house h^i is a maximizer of

$\ln(v^i(x^i)) - p_{x^i}$, and therefore, it is also a maximizer of $v^i(x^i)/e^{p_{x^i}}$. Thus, $\langle(\lambda_h = 1/e^{p_h})_{h \in H}, (h^i)_{i \in N}\rangle$ constitutes a biased preferences equilibrium.

In the other direction, let $\langle\lambda, (h^i)\rangle$ be a biased preferences equilibrium and (x^i) be any other assignment. For each i, $\lambda_{h^i} v^i(h^i) \geq \lambda_{x^i} v^i(x^i)$ and therefore, $\Pi_i \lambda_{h^i} v^i(h^i) \geq \Pi_i \lambda_{x^i} v^i(x^i)$. Since $\Pi_i \lambda_{h^i} = \Pi_i \lambda_{x^i}$, it follows that $\Pi_i v^i(h^i) \geq \Pi_i v^i(x^i)$, that is, (h^i) is Nash maximal.

We proceed with two modifications to the housing economy:

Example: The Partnership Economy

As in Shapley and Shubik (1971), the agents are composed of two equally-sized populations, A and B. Each agent chooses a unique partner from the other population, that is, $X^i = B$ for any $i \in A$ and $X^j = A$ for any $j \in B$. A profile is feasible if for every i, j, if i chooses j, then j chooses i. An agent i's valuation of a partnership with j is $v^i(j) > 0$. Importantly, the ex-ante valuations are assumed to be symmetric, that is, $v^i(j) = v^j(i)$, but the biased valuations might not be.

Example: Let $A = \{1, 2\}$ and $B = \{3, 4\}$. Table 4.3 presents the original valuations (left bi-matrix) and the equilibrium biased valuations (right bi-matrix). Each cell gives the values of i and j of being matched. The Nash-maximal matching is $1 \leftrightarrow 4$ and $2 \leftrightarrow 3$ (depicted), which is a biased preferences equilibrium with the bias $\lambda = (2, 1, 2, 1)$.

	3	4
1	1,1	3,3
2	3,3	4,4

$T(\cdot, \lambda) \longrightarrow$

	3	4
1	2,2	3,6
2	6,3	4,4

Table 4.3 A Biased Preferences Equilibrium

Claim: In the partnership economy, the set of biased preferences equilibrium outcomes is the set of all Nash-maximal profiles.

Proof: Let (a^i) be a Nash-maximal profile, that is, one that maximizes $\Sigma_{i \in N} \ln(v^i(x^i))$ over F. Since the utility functions are symmetric, i.e. $(v^i(j) = v^j(i))$, the profile (a^i) also maximizes both $\Sigma_{i \in A} \ln(v^i(x^i))$ and $\Sigma_{i \in B} \ln(v^i(x^i))$ over F. Taking the agents to be A and the houses to be B, Shapley and Shubik (1971) showed that a price vector $(p_j)_{j \in B}$ exists, such that for every agent $i \in A$, the choice of a^i maximizes $\ln(v^i(j)) - p_j$ over all $j \in X^i = B$ and therefore, maximizes $v^i(j)/e^{p_j}$ as well. Reversing roles, there is a price vector $(p_j)_{j \in A}$ with analogous optimality properties. Therefore, $\langle (\lambda_j = 1/e^{p_j})_{j \in N}, (a^i)_{i \in N} \rangle$ constitutes a biased preferences equilibrium.

In the other direction, let $\langle (\lambda_j)_{j \in N}, (a^i)_{i \in N} \rangle$ be a biased preferences equilibrium, and let $(x^i) \in F$. For every i, it holds that $\lambda_{a^i} v^i(a^i) \geq \lambda_{x^i} v^i(x^i)$. Therefore, $\Pi_i[\lambda_{a^i} v^i(a^i)] \geq \Pi_i[\lambda_{x^i} v^i(x^i)]$. Since $\Pi_i \lambda_{a^i} = \Pi_i \lambda_{x^i}$, it follows that $\Pi_i v^i(a^i) \geq \Pi_i v^i(x^i)$. That is, (a^i) is Nash maximal. ∎

The condition that the value of a match between any two agents is the same for both of them is sufficient for the A-Nash-maximal matching to be B-Nash-maximal as well. Without this condition, a biased preferences equilibrium may not exist:

Example: Consider an assignment economy where $A = \{1, 2\}$, $B = \{3, 4\}$, and $3 \succ^1 4$, $1 \succ^4 2$, $4 \succ^2 3$, $2 \succ^3 1$. No utility presentation of these preferences is consistent with the assumption that the value of a match is identical for both partners (since it requires that $v^1(3) > v^1(4) = v^4(1) > v^4(2) = v^2(4) > v^2(3) = v^3(2) > v^3(1) = v^1(3)$).

Suppose that $1 \leftrightarrow 3$ is a match in a biased preferences equilibrium. Then, $\lambda_1 > \lambda_2$ (so that agent 3 chooses agent 1 over agent 2). But then, agent 4 will also choose agent 1, violating feasibility. Likewise, $1 \leftrightarrow 4$ cannot be a match in a biased preferences equilibrium.

Example: A Production Economy

In the production economy (related to Atakan et al. (2023)), there is a set of indivisible goods K and two equally-sized groups of agents: *consumers* (C) and *producers* (P). Every $i \in C$ consumes exactly one unit of a single good, that is $X^i = K$, and $u_k^i > 0$ is consumer i's utility from consuming good k (which he wishes to *maximize*). Every producer $i \in P$ *must* produce exactly one unit of a single good, that is, $X^i = K$, and $c_k^i > 0$ is producer i's *utility-cost* from producing good k (which he wishes to *minimize*). The set F consists of all profiles satisfying that, for every good k, the number of its consumers is equal to the number of its producers. Note that this economy differs from the partnership economy in that consumers and producers choose a good rather than a partner and the biases are applied to the goods rather than to the agents.

A bias vector $\lambda = (\lambda_k)_{k \in K}$ alters consumer i's utility vector from $(u_k^i)_{k \in K}$ to $(\lambda_k u_k^i)_{k \in K}$ and producer i's utility-cost vector from $(c_k^i)_{k \in K}$ to $(\lambda_k c_k^i)_{k \in K}$. Thus, a bias λ simultaneously rescales both the consumers' utility and the producers' utility-costs of good k by the same factor λ_k. Thus, an *increase* in λ_k is analogous to that of a *decrease* in the price of good k in a regular exchange economy: it makes the good more desirable to buyers and less desirable to sellers. Underlying a bias could be some trait such as quality: a high bias, like a high quality level, makes the good more desirable to consumers and increases the utility-cost to produce it.

The following claim again uses a Shapley and Shubik (1971)-style argument to characterize the biased preferences equilibrium profiles. It implies that they exist and are pre-Pareto optimal.

Claim: In the production economy, the biased preferences equilibrium profiles are precisely the solutions of:

$$\max_{(x^i) \in F} \frac{\prod\limits_{i \in C} u_{x^i}^i}{\prod\limits_{i \in P} c_{x^i}^i} \tag{*}$$

Proof: Let $\langle \lambda, (x^i) \rangle$ be a biased preferences equilibrium, and let $(y^i) \in F$. It follows that $\lambda_{x^i} u^i_{x^i} \geq \lambda_{y^i} u^i_{y^i}$ for every $i \in C$ and $\lambda_{x^i} c^i_{x^i} \leq \lambda_{y^i} c^i_{y^i}$ for every $i \in P$. Combined with the equality $\Pi_{i \in C} \lambda_{z^i} = \Pi_{i \in P} \lambda_{z^i}$, which holds for all $(z^i) \in F$, we conclude that:

$$\frac{\underset{i \in C}{\Pi}\, u^i_{x^i}}{\underset{i \in P}{\Pi}\, c^i_{x^i}} = \frac{\underset{i \in C}{\Pi}\, \lambda_{x^i} u^i_{x^i}}{\underset{i \in P}{\Pi}\, \lambda_{x^i} c^i_{x^i}} \geq \frac{\underset{i \in C}{\Pi}\, \lambda_{y^i} u^i_{y^i}}{\underset{i \in P}{\Pi}\, \lambda_{y^i} c^i_{y^i}} = \frac{\underset{i \in C}{\Pi}\, u^i_{y^i}}{\underset{i \in P}{\Pi}\, c^i_{y^i}}$$

and therefore (x^i) is a solution of (*).

In the other direction, let (x^i) be a solution of (*). Let (x^i_k) be the allocation matrix with a row for each agent and a column for each good, where $x^i_k = 1$ if i chooses k and $x^i_k = 0$ otherwise. The matrix solves the following linear maximization problem:

$$\max_{(m^i_k)} \Sigma_k \Sigma_{i \in C} [\ln(u^i_k) m^i_k] + \Sigma_k \Sigma_{i \in P} [-\ln(c^i_k) m^i_k]$$

such that

$$\Sigma_{i \in C} m^i_k - \Sigma_{i \in P} m^i_k = 0 \; \forall k \qquad (\mu_k)$$

$$m^i_k \geq 0 \; \forall i, k \qquad (\gamma^i_k)$$

$$\Sigma_k m^i_k = 1 \; \forall i \qquad (\psi^i)$$

The above problem always has a solution which is a binary matrix (that is, $x^i_k = 0$ or 1, for every i, k). To understand why, Birkhoff (1946) (and his extensions in Budish et al. (2013)) shows that any matrix of real numbers that satisfies the above constraints is a convex combination of binary matrices that also satisfy them. Since the target function is linear, any such binary matrix is also a solution to the linear programming problem.

The constraints in the above optimization are labelled by their shadow values, which appear in the parenthesis to the right. Let $\lambda = (e^{\mu_k})_{k \in K}$. We will now verify that $\langle \lambda, (x^i) \rangle$ is a biased preferences equilibrium.

The matrix (x^i_k) satisfies the following conditions for every $i \in C$ and $k \in K$:

$$\ln(u^i_k)+\mu_k+\gamma^i_k+\psi^i=0,\ \gamma^i_k x^i_k=0 \text{ and } \gamma^i_k \le 0$$

If $x^i_k=1$, then for any $k' \in K: \ln(u^i_k)+\mu_k+\psi^i=0 \ge \ln(u^i_{k'})+\mu_{k'}+\psi^i$ and therefore, $\lambda_k u^i_k \ge \lambda_{k'} u^i_{k'}$, that is, k is i's most preferred good according to the λ-biased preferences. Likewise, for every $i \in P$ and $k \in K$:

$$-\ln(c^i_k)-\mu_k+\gamma^i_k+\psi^i=0,\ \gamma^i_k x^i_k=0 \text{ and } \gamma^i_k \le 0$$

If $x^i_k=1$, then for any $k': -\ln(c^i_k)-\mu_k+\psi^i=0 \ge -\ln(c^i_{k'})-\mu_{k'}+\psi^i$ and therefore, $c^i_k \lambda_k \le c^i_{k'}\lambda_{k'}$, that is, k minimizes i's λ-biased utility-costs. ∎

Example: Table 4.4 (left panel) depicts a production economy with two goods, two consumers (C1 and C2), and two producers (P1 and P2). The right panel indicates a biased preferences equilibrium with $\lambda=(1,3)$ where Consumer 1 and Producer 1 choose Good 1, and Consumer 2 and Producer 2 choose Good 2.

	Good 1	Good 2			1· Good 1	3· Good 2
C1	4	1	$T(\cdot,\lambda)$	C1	4	3
C2	4	2		C2	4	6
P1	2	1		P1	2	3
P2	4	1		P2	4	3

Table 4.4 A Biased Preferences Equilibrium in a Production Economy. The left panel presents the initial utilities and utility-costs for the agents and the right panel presents the biased utilities and utility-costs with the bias $\lambda=(1,3)$.

Initially, both consumers prefer to consume good 1, while both producers prefer to produce good 2. In the solution of (*) (with the value $(4\cdot 2)/(2\cdot 1)$), C1 and P1 choose good 1, and C2 and P2 choose good 2. This outcome is obtained in equilibrium by, for example, $\lambda=(1,3)$, a bias that induces one consumer to switch from good 1 to good 2, and one producer to switch from good 2 to good 1.

5 A Comparison to Game Theory

In this final chapter, we compare this book's modelling approaches to those of standard Game Theory. Rather than talking abstractly, we make the comparison more concrete by considering two specific "battlegrounds". In both, we contrast our solution concepts with the standard ones. As always, we *do not* argue positively or normatively in favour of adopting the social institutions underlying any of these solution concepts. Rather, we simply wish to encourage readers to abandon the dogmatic use of familiar solution concepts and to consider less conventional frameworks.

The first battleground is the matching economy. It involves a single even-numbered population of agents who must match into exclusive pairs, which we refer to as a *pairing*. Each agent is characterized by a preference relation over potential mates. A special case is Gale and Shapley (1962)'s two-sided matching problem, one of the most iconic models in Economic Theory. In that problem, the agents are partitioned into two equal-sized groups, and each agent prefers to be matched with any agent from the other group over being matched with an agent from his own group.

The standard cooperative game-theoretical solution concept for matching economies is "pairwise stability", which is a pairing for which there are no two agents in different pairs who prefer each other over their current partners. Following Richter and Rubinstein (2024), we compare this concept with three of the approaches discussed in this book (modified to fit the matching problem):

- The *jungle equilibrium* in which a power relation governs society.
- The *Y-equilibrium* in which society is governed by norms that specify what is permissible and what is forbidden.
- The *status and initial status equilibrium* concepts in which a status ordering upholds harmony in a society.

 https://doi.org/10.11647/OBP.0404.05

The second battleground is a "political economy" situation. There is a group of agents with views on a political issue. Each agent chooses a position and has preferences only regarding the position he himself chooses (and not the outcome of the process). There is a need that a majority of agents choose the same position. If there is no majority position, then a crisis ensues.

Traditionally, such a situation is modelled as a non-cooperative game, and its *Nash equilibria* are calculated. Extending Richter and Rubinstein (2021), we compare this approach with two of the approaches discussed in this book:

• The *convex Y-equilibrium* in which society is governed by (convex) norms that specify what is permissible and what is forbidden.
• The *biased preferences equilibria* where preferences are systematically biased.

In both battlegrounds, the matching problem and the political economy setting, we will see that the new approaches lead to very different outcomes than the traditional ones.

5.1   The Matching Economy

In the matching economy, N is an even-numbered population of n agents. The set of alternatives is taken to be the set of agents, i.e. $X = N$. A *pairing* is a profile $(x^i)_{i \in N}$ that specifies, for every i, a partner $x^i \neq i$, such that if i is paired with j, then j is paired with i. The feasibility set F is the set of all pairings. Note that F is not closed under permutations (if i and j exchange partners, then feasibility requires that x^i and x^j also exchange partners). A match between two agents i and j is denoted as $i \mapsto j$. We assume that agents prefer to have any partner over being alone; in other words, every agent bottom-ranks himself. Therefore, it will be sufficient to specify, for each agent i, a strict preference relation $\succ^i$ over $X\backslash\{i\}$, the set of all *other* agents.

As mentioned, the standard solution concept for this economy is pairwise stability, which is a pairing such that there are no two agents in different pairs who prefer each other over their respective current partners. Formally, a pairing (x^i) is *pairwise stable* if there is no i and j such that $j \succ^i x^i$ and $i \succ^j x^j$.

The *two-sided matching economy* is a special case of the matching economy. The set of agents N is partitioned into two equally-sized sets, N_1 and N_2, and every agent prefers any agent from the other group over any agent from his own group. We say that a pairing is *mixed* if every couple has a member from each group. For two-sided matching economies, a pairwise-stable pairing always exists and can be calculated using Gale and Shapley (1962)'s deferred acceptance algorithm. However, in the general matching economy, a pairwise-stable pairing often does not exist. The following is Gale and Shapley (1962)'s canonical example of a matching economy with no pairwise-stable pairing:

Agent	1	2	3	4
1st Preference	2	3	1	1
2nd Preference	3	1	2	2
3rd Preference	4	4	4	3

Table 5.1 A matching economy with no pairwise-stable pairing.

To see that there is no pairwise-stable pairing, consider a candidate pairing. Let i be the agent matched with 4. Agent i prefers every other agent over 4, and there is an agent $j \in \{1, 2, 3\} \setminus \{i\}$ who top-ranks i. Thus, the couple $i \leftrightarrow j$ blocks the candidate pairing from being pairwise stable.

As discussed in Section 0.4, we distinguish between two types of equilibrium concepts: the choice type (like competitive equilibrium) and the deviation type (like Nash equilibrium). Two of the concepts which we will apply, the Y-equilibrium and the initial status equilibrium, belong to the choice type. In these solution concepts, some internally determined parameter will restrict every agent's choice set so that there is a pairing in which every agent's partner is his most preferred from his choice set.

The other solution concepts that we apply to the matching problem belong to the deviation type. An equilibrium concept of this type captures immunity against certain threats that would "rock the boat". A prominent example is pairwise stability where the threat is the existence of the mutual interest of two agents in abandoning their current partner to form a new match.

We have a different unilateral threat in mind: for harmony to be disturbed, it is sufficient that one agent is willing and able to approach another agent. The threat is merely the *approach* of an agent to someone who is not his partner, whether or not his approach is reciprocated.

The perspective of life which we model is that a pairing can be destabilized not by coalitions but merely by an agent A approaching an agent B (who is not matched with A) and expressing his desire for B to abandon his current partner and match with him instead. This destabilizes society regardless of whether or not B reciprocates A's affections. Why does A approach B? Actually, why not? He might know that B also prefers him over B's current partner (which is the premise of pairwise stability). Even if he knows that B does not prefer him, A might hope that if he approaches B, then B will feel flattered and change his opinion. Finally, A might not know B's preferences and simply tries his luck.

Generally, it is impossible for every agent to be paired with his top choice because agents' desires are not perfectly reciprocated. Therefore, achieving stability when agents can make unilateral approaches requires restrictions on which approaches are allowed. Given such restrictions, we say that a pairing is *unilaterally stable* if there is no agent who wishes to approach another and is able to do so. A familiar and very strict social norm forbids approaching any matched individual. Such a norm achieves harmony in a society, but at the cost of drastically restricting personal freedom. The restrictions described in the following three sections involve social institutions (power, taboos, and status) that limit an agent's ability to act, but in a less draconian manner.

The following is a running example which will be used to illustrate the different solution concepts:

Example: The Common-ranking Two-sided Matching Economy

A *common-ranking two-sided matching economy* is a two-sided matching economy where every agent in N_1 ranks members of N_2 according to a common ranking $j_1 \succ_2 j_2 \succ_2 \ldots \succ_2 j_{n/2}$, and every agent in N_2 ranks his potential partners in N_1 according to $i_1 \succ_1 i_2 \succ_1 \ldots \succ_1 i_{n/2}$.

In such an economy, the set of Pareto-optimal pairings is the set of all mixed pairings (recall that, a pairing is mixed if each agent is paired with an agent from the other side). To see why, any pairing that matches two members of the same side also matches two members from the other side. However, in that case, all four agents can be beneficially re-paired with members of the other side, making a Pareto improvement. On the other hand, in any mixed matching, improving one agent's situation requires moving another agent down the common preference ladder, so no Pareto improvements can exist.

5.2 The Jungle Equilibrium

The first solution concept we apply is related to the jungle model described in Chapter 1 with the key difference being that the power ordering is endogenous. An equilibrium candidate is a tuple $\langle \rhd, (x^i) \rangle$ where (x^i) is a pairing and $\rhd$ is a strict ordering on N. The statement $i \rhd j$ means that i is more powerful than j. We consider three variants of the jungle equilibrium which differ in what circumstances power prevents an agent from approaching another agent. In particular, in a J1-equilibrium an agent is only able to approach agents who are weaker than himself. In a J2-equilibrium, an agent needs to be stronger than both the agent he is approaching and that agent's current partner. In a J3-equilibrium, an agent also needs to be stronger than his own partner.

As mentioned and unlike in Chapter 1, the power relation here is part of the description of an equilibrium (as in Rubinstein and Yıldız (2022)). This is akin to competitive equilibrium where prices are determined in equilibrium.

Definition: J1-Equilibrium

A *J1-equilibrium* is a tuple $\langle \rhd, (x^i) \rangle$ in which there are no two agents i and j such that i prefers j over his current partner (that is, $j \succ^i x^i$) and i is more powerful than j (that is, $i \rhd j$).

In a J1-equilibrium pairing, it can be that an agent prefers another to his current partner. But, the agent is prohibited from making such an approach because the agent to be approached is stronger than him. This contrasts with pairwise stability where what prevents him from acting is that the agent to be approached will reject him.

The following proposition compares the J1-equilibrium concept with that of pairwise stability. It is found that the J1-equilibrium concept is stricter: any J1-equilibrium outcome is pairwise stable (and therefore also Pareto-optimal). Since pairwise-stable pairings do not always exist, neither will J1-equilibria.

Proposition 5.1: J1-equilibrium Properties

(i) Every J1-equilibrium pairing is pairwise stable.

(ii) A pairwise-stable pairing might not be a J1-equilibrium pairing.

Proof:

(i) Let $\langle \rhd, (x^i) \rangle$ be a J1-equilibrium. Suppose that there are two agents i and j who strictly prefer each other to their current partners. One of them must be $\rhd$-stronger than the other, and he prefers the weaker agent over his current partner, thus violating the J1-equilibrium condition.

(ii) In a J1-equilibrium, the strongest agent is matched with his first-best choice. In the following matching economy, the pairing $1 \leftrightarrow 2$ and $3 \leftrightarrow 4$ is pairwise stable, but there is no agent who is matched with his first best:

Agent	1	2	3	4
1st Preference	4	3	1	2
2nd Preference	2	1	4	3
3rd Preference	3	4	2	1

Table 5.2 Preferences with a pairwise-stable pairing (highlighted) that is not a J1-equilibrium outcome.

Example: The Common-ranking Two-sided Matching Economy

The pairing $\{i_1 \leftrightarrow j_1, i_2 \leftrightarrow j_2, \cdots, i_{n/2} \leftrightarrow j_{n/2}\}$ combined with any power ordering $\triangleright$ that satisfies $i_1, j_1 \triangleright i_2, j_2 \triangleright \cdots \triangleright i_{n/2}, j_{n/2}$ is a J1-equilibrium. There is no other J1-equilibrium pairing: Since every agent in N_2 top-ranks i_1, agent i_1 must be stronger than everyone in N_2 except perhaps his partner. This means that, in any equilibrium, i_1 has to be matched with his first-best, namely j_1. Similarly, j_1 must be stronger than all members of N_1, except possibly i_1. This pattern continues down the ranking. Among the remaining agents, i_2 and j_2 are matched, and i_2 must be more powerful than $\{j_3, \ldots, j_{n/2}\}$ while j_2 must be stronger than $\{i_3, \ldots, i_{n/2}\}$ and so on.

In the jungle model (Chapter 1), the ability of one agent to take the house of another and, likewise, in a J1-equilibrium the ability of one agent to approach another, depends solely on the power relationship between the two agents. However, in the context of the matching economy, any approach involves not only the agent who initiates the approach and the approached agent but also their partners. The following two solution concepts take this into account. In a J2-equilibrium, an agent can approach another in a different pair only if he is stronger than both the desired agent *and* that agent's partner.

Definition: J2-Equilibrium

A *J2-equilibrium* is a tuple $\langle \triangleright, (x^i) \rangle$ in which there are no two agents i and j such that i prefers j over his current partner (that is, $j \succ^i x^i$) and is more powerful than *both* j and j's partner (that is, $i \triangleright j$ and $i \triangleright x^j$).

Like the J1-equilibrium, the J2-equilibrium does not allow for pairings in which no agent gets his first best: in any J2-equilibrium, the strongest agent is matched with his most-preferred partner. Obviously, every J1-equilibrium is also a J2-equilibrium. We will now see that a J2-equilibrium always exists, unlike a J1-equilibrium.

Proposition 5.2: J2-equilibrium Properties

(i) A J2-equilibrium always exists.

(ii) Every J2-equilibrium pairing is Pareto-optimal.

(iii) A Pareto-optimal pairing (even if it is pairwise stable) need not be a J2-equilibrium pairing.

Proof:

(i) Choose an arbitrary agent i_1, and make him the strongest agent. Call his first-best partner j_1, pair them together, and make j_1 the weakest agent. Continue in this manner to obtain a pairing in which every agent i_k is paired with j_k, who is i_k's favourite partner from $N - \{i_1, j_1, \ldots, i_{k-1}, j_{k-1}\}$, and set the power relation to be $i_1 \triangleright i_2 \triangleright \cdots \triangleright j_2 \triangleright j_1$. Thus, every i_k is stronger than every j_l.

This procedure generates a J2-equilibrium. Any agent who might be preferred by i_k over j_k must have been paired earlier, and thus, is either stronger than i_k or has a partner who is. No j_l can approach any other agent because every other couple, $i_k \leftrightarrow j_k$, has at least one member who is stronger than him, namely i_k.

(ii) Let $\langle \triangleright, (x^i) \rangle$ be a J2-equilibrium. Assume that (y^i) Pareto-dominates (x^i). Let j be the strongest agent in $D \equiv \{i \mid x^i \neq y^i\}$. By Pareto-dominance, $y^j \succ^j x^j$ (recall that preferences are strict). Agent y^j and y^j's original partner x^{y^j} are both in D. Therefore, $j \triangleright y^j, x^{y^j}$, which violates $\langle \triangleright, (x^i) \rangle$ being a J2-equilibrium.

(iii) For the economy depicted in Table 5.2, the highlighted pairing $\{1 \leftrightarrow 2, 3 \leftrightarrow 4\}$ is pairwise stable but is not a J2-equilibrium pairing since no agent gets his first-best.

Example: The Common-ranking Two-sided Matching Economy

Every mixed pairing (x^i) is a J2-equilibrium pairing supported by assigning the power relations of agents in each side by the rank of their matches (that is, for every two members i and j from the same side assign $i \triangleright j$ if x^i is higher-ranked than x^j).

While every mixed pairing is part of a J2-equilibrium, not every power relation is. For example, for the case of four agents, there is no J2-equilibrium with the power relation $j_2 \triangleright i_1 \triangleright i_2 \triangleright j_1$. This is because j_2 is the most powerful, and must be matched with i_1. Thus, the only candidate pairing is $\{i_1 \hookrightarrow j_2, i_2 \hookrightarrow j_1\}$. But this is not a J2-equilibrium because i_1 prefers j_1 over j_2, and is stronger than both i_2 and j_1.

Finally, in a J3-equilibrium, an agent can force a partnership with j only if he is stronger than j, j's partner, and his own abandoned partner.

Definition: J3-Equilibrium

A *J3-equilibrium* is a tuple $\langle \triangleright, (x^i) \rangle$ for which there are no i and j such that $j \succ^i x^i$ and $i \triangleright j, x^i, x^j$.

Obviously, every J2-equilibrium is also a J3-equilibrium. The J3-equilibrium requires stronger conditions for an agent to be able to disturb society's harmony, and we will see that every power relation is part of some J3-equilibrium (unlike the J2-equilibrium case). Nonetheless, in terms of equilibrium pairings, the J2- and J3-equilibrium notions are equivalent.

Proposition 5.3: J3-equilibrium Properties

(i) For every power relation $\triangleright$, there is a J3-equilibrium $\langle \triangleright, (x^i) \rangle$.

(ii) The set of J3-equilibrium pairings is equal to the set of J2-equilibrium pairings (thus, every J3-equilibrium pairing is Pareto-optimal, though not every Pareto-optimal pairing is a J3-equilibrium pairing).

Proof:

(i) Let $\triangleright$ be a strict ordering. We inductively construct a pairing (x^i) for which $\langle \triangleright, (x^i) \rangle$ is a J3-equilibrium using a "generalized serial dictatorship" procedure: First, the $\triangleright$-strongest agent picks his most-preferred partner and they are matched. In each subsequent step, the $\triangleright$-strongest remaining agent is matched with his most-preferred partner from among those remaining. By this procedure, half of the agents "make a choice" while the other half "are chosen". Any agent who "makes a choice" can only prefer agents who match before him, i.e. those who are stronger than him or are paired with a stronger partner. Any agent who "is chosen" is neutralized because he is matched with a stronger partner.

(ii) As mentioned, any J2-equilibrium is also a J3-equilibrium. We now show that any J3-equilibrium pairing is a J2-equilibrium pairing (perhaps with a different power relation). Consider a J3-equilibrium $\langle \triangleright, (x^i) \rangle$. In every couple, there is a stronger agent and a weaker one. Let S be the set of $n/2$ stronger agents and W be the set of $n/2$ weaker ones. Define a new power relation $\triangleright'$ by preserving $\triangleright$ on S and on W and pushing all members of W below all members of S. The tuple $\langle \triangleright', (x^i) \rangle$ is a J2-equilibrium: If not, then there would be i and j such that $j \succ^i x^i$ and $i \triangleright' x^j, j$. It must be that $i \in S$ since i is $\triangleright'$-stronger than a pair of agents, $j \mapsto x^j$. Thus, $i \triangleright x^i$. Since the power relation is preserved on S, i is $\triangleright$-stronger than the $\triangleright$-stronger agent in $\{j, x^j\}$ who is in S. Thus, $i \triangleright x^i, j, x^j$, contradicting $\langle \triangleright, (x^i) \rangle$ being a J3-equilibrium.

5.3   Restricting Partnerships: Pairwise Y-equilibrium

We now adjust the Y-equilibrium concept (Chapter 2) to fit the matching economy. Since every agent needs a partner, uniformly restricting the set of permitted partners will leave some agents without a partner. Instead, the social norm determines which *pairs* are permitted and which are forbidden.

> ### Definition: Y-Equilibrium
>
> Let M be the set of all doubletons (sets of size 2). A *para-Y-equilibrium* is a tuple $\langle Y,(x^i)\rangle$ where $Y \subseteq M$ and (x^i) is a pairing such that, for every agent i, x^i is $\succ^i$-maximal in $\{j \mid \{i,j\} \in Y\}$. A *Y-equilibrium* is a para-Y-equilibrium such that there is no other para-Y-equilibrium $\langle Z,(y^i)\rangle$ with $Y \subset Z$.

Any set of permissible pairs Y induces, for each agent i, a choice set of permissible partners $\{j \mid \{i,j\} \in Y\}$. Thus, unlike the Y-equilibrium notion of Chapter 2, here the Y-equilibrium notion treats agents asymmetrically in the sense that different agents face different choice sets with the restriction that if j is permissible for i, then i is also permissible for j. The adapted Y-equilibrium notion requires that, for any larger permissible set, there is an i and j such that i would choose j but j would not choose i.

The following proposition shows that the set of Y-equilibrium pairings is the set of all Pareto-optimal pairings. This implies that, in term of outcomes, the Y-equilibrium notion is more permissive than pairwise stability or the J-equilibrium notions. In particular, it always exists.

> ### Proposition 5.4: Y-equilibrium and Pareto Optimality
>
> The set of Y-equilibrium pairings $=$ The set of Pareto-optimal pairings.

> ### Proof:
>
> Given any pairing (x^i), define $L((x^i))$ to be the set of all doubletons $\{i,j\}$ such that $x^i \succsim^i j$ and $x^j \succsim^j i$. Notice that for every i, the doubleton $\{i, x^i\}$ is in $L((x^i))$.
>
> Let $\langle Y,(x^i)\rangle$ be a Y-equilibrium and (y^i) be a pairing that Pareto-dominates (x^i). Obviously, $L((x^i)) \supseteq Y$. Clearly, $L((y^i)) \supseteq L((x^i))$. In fact, the inclusion is strict since at least one agent, say j, is strictly better off in (y^i) and therefore the pair $\{j, y^j\}$ is in $L((y^i)) - L((x^i))$. The

tuple $\langle L((y^i)), (y^i) \rangle$ is a para-Y-equilibrium with a larger set of permissible pairs, which contradicts $\langle Y, (x^i) \rangle$ being a Y-equilibrium.

On the other hand, let (x^i) be a Pareto-optimal pairing. We now show that the tuple $\langle L((x^i)), (x^i) \rangle$ is a Y-equilibrium. If not, then there is a para-Y-equilibrium $\langle Z, (y^i) \rangle$ with $Z \supset L((x^i))$. All agents are weakly better off in (y^i) than in (x^i). The set Z contains at least one pair $\{i, j\}$ which is not in $L((x^i))$. Without loss of generality, suppose that $j \succ^i x^i$. In that case, $y^i \succsim^i j \succ^i x^i$ and therefore, (y^i) Pareto-dominates (x^i).

Example: The Common-ranking Two-sided Matching Economy

Every mixed pairing is Pareto-optimal and therefore, is a Y-equilibrium pairing. The Y-equilibrium pairing $\{i_1 \hookrightarrow j_1, i_2 \hookrightarrow j_2, \ldots\}$ is supported by a maximally restricted permissible set which contains only the equilibrium matches (and all the matches between any two agents from the same side).

5.4   Prestige by Partner: Status Equilibrium

We now turn to the status equilibrium concept discussed in Chapter 3 (referred to as an S-equilibrium in Richter and Rubinstein (2024)). Harmony is established by a status ordering of the agents that blocks an agent from approaching certain other agents. In a status equilibrium, agents are paired up, and *no agent can approach any other agent who has a higher status than his current partner.* The only agents he has the courage to approach are those with a (weakly) lower status than his own partner. An equilibrium is harmonious in that no agent can find a different partner who is both approachable and more desirable.

> ### Definition: Status Equilibrium
>
> A status equilibrium is a tuple $\langle P, (x^i) \rangle$ where (x^i) is a pairing and P is a weak ordering of the agents such that, for every agent i, there is no j such that $j \succ^i x^i$ and $x^i P j$.

Status equilibrium pairings have the properties that at least one agent (the agent with the highest-ranked partner) gets a partner whom he most prefers, and if preferences are strict, then at most one agent gets his least-preferred partner (it can only be the agent with the lowest-ranked partner).

We now establish some relationships between the status equilibrium concept and the J2-equilibrium, Pareto optimality, and pairwise stability.

> ### Proposition 5.5: Status Equilibrium Properties
>
> (i) Every status equilibrium pairing is a J2-equilibrium pairing and therefore, is Pareto-optimal.
>
> (ii) The notions of status equilibrium and pairwise-stability are distinct; it is possible for either notion to exist when the other one does not.

> ### Proof:
>
> (i) Let $\langle P, (x^i) \rangle$ be a status equilibrium and break ties so that P is strict. Define a power ranking $\triangleright$ by ranking agents according to the status of their partners: $i \triangleright j$ if $x^i P x^j$. The tuple $\langle \triangleright, (x^i) \rangle$ is a J2-equilibrium: If $j \succ^i x^i$ for some i, j, then it must be that $j P x^i$ since $\langle \triangleright, (x^i) \rangle$ is a status equilibrium. But then $x^j \triangleright i$, and i is prevented from approaching j by the power of j's partner. By Proposition 5.2, the pairing is also Pareto-optimal.
>
> (ii) In the economy depicted in Table 5.1, there is no pairwise-stable pairing, but the ordering $1 P 2 P 3 P 4$ supports the pairings $\{1 \leftrightarrow 3, 2 \leftrightarrow 4\}$ and $\{1 \leftrightarrow 4, 2 \leftrightarrow 3\}$ as status equilibria.

In the economy depicted in Table 5.2, the highlighted pairing $\{1\leftrightarrow2, 3\leftrightarrow4\}$ is pairwise stable, but there is no status equilibrium: The highlighted pairing is not a status equilibrium pairing because no agent gets his first-best. Neither are the other two pairings because in each of them, two agents get their last choice.

Example: The Common-ranking Two-sided Matching Economy

By Proposition 5.5, only mixed pairings can be status equilibrium pairings. In fact, *any mixed pairing* is a status equilibrium pairing with any ranking P that satisfies $i_1 P i_2 P \ldots P i_{n/2}$ and $j_1 P j_2 P \ldots P j_{n/2}$ (for any agent i, every agent that i desires more than his partner has a higher status than i's partner).

5.5   Prestige by Self: Initial Status Equilibrium

We adapt the initial status equilibrium concept to the matching economy by taking an agent's initial status to be himself. Recall that this concept belongs to the choice group of solution concepts (see Section 0.4). Every agent chooses his partner, but the status ranking only allows an agent to approach agents with the same status or lower. In equilibrium, the status ranking is such that the individual choices form a pairing (that is, if i chooses j, then j chooses i). Formally, a candidate for an initial status equilibrium is a tuple $\langle P,(x^i)\rangle$ where iPj is interpreted as "i's status is at least as high as j's" and (x^i) is a pairing. This adapted initial status equilibrium concept is referred to as a C-equilibrium in Richter and Rubinstein (2024).

Definition: Initial Status Equilibrium

An initial status equilibrium is a tuple $\langle P,(x^i)\rangle$ such that, for every agent i, his partner x^i is i's most-preferred partner in $\{j \in N \mid iPj\}$.

Obviously, any two matched agents in an initial status equilibrium must have the same status. Therefore, every initial status equilibrium is also a status equilibrium and, by Proposition 5.5, its pairing is Pareto-optimal.

Of particular interest is the relationship between the initial status equilibrium and the J1-equilibrium. If $\langle P, (x^i) \rangle$ is an initial status equilibrium, then $\langle \triangleright, (x^i) \rangle$ is a J1-equilibrium where $\triangleright$ is any strict tie-breaking of P (that is, $i \triangleright j$ only if $i P j$).

However, unlike the initial status equilibrium concept, a J1-equilibrium does not require that an agent be weakly stronger than his partner. Many pairings can be a J1-equilibrium pairing but not an initial status equilibrium pairing. For example, consider the two-sided matching economy with $N_1 = \{1, 3\}$, $N_2 = \{2, 4\}$, and a tragedy: 1 loves 2, 2 loves 3, 3 loves 4, and 4 loves 1. Both mixed pairings are J1-equilibrium pairings. One is the first-best for N_1's members. It is supported by any power relation that ranks N_1's members above N_2's members. The other is the opposite. Neither is an initial status equilibrium pairing (shortly, we will see why).

We need an additional concept. We say that the matching economy is *pair-rankable* if the set of agents N can be partitioned into doubletons $I_1, \ldots, I_{n/2}$, such that each agent in I_q prefers his partner in the doubleton to any member of $I_{q+1} \cup \cdots \cup I_{n/2}$. In other words, the agents can be partitioned into a sequence of doubletons where every agent's partner is his best choice from those who are not ahead of him.

Pair-rankability is a strong property of a matching economy which emerges in some natural settings. Two classical families of pair-rankable matching economies are:

(i) Agents live in a metric space and rank partners by their closeness. The first doubleton can consist of the two closest agents, and each subsequent doubleton consists of the two closest among those remaining.

(ii) Agents are positioned on a line, and each has single-peaked preferences over the other agents with a peak at one of his neighbours. This implies that an extreme agent top-ranks his only neighbour and, for any set of agents, there are two neighbours such that the left one top-ranks his right neighbour while the right one top-ranks his left neighbour.

> ### Proposition 5.6: Initial Status Equilibrium Properties
>
> (i) A matching economy has an initial status equilibrium if and only if it is pair-rankable.
>
> (ii) If an initial status equilibrium pairing exists, then it is unique and pairwise stable.

> ### Proof:
>
> (i) Let $\langle P, (x^i) \rangle$ be an initial status equilibrium. An agent who is P-maximal must be matched with someone who is also P-maximal. Thus, both must like each other more than they like anyone else. Denote this doubleton as I_1. Among the agents outside of I_1, there is an agent who is P-maximal. Again, he and his partner are equally ranked and therefore, both must prefer each other to anyone else in $N - I_1$, and so on. Thus, the existence of an initial status equilibrium requires that the economy is pair-rankable.
>
> In the other direction, let $I_1, \ldots, I_{n/2}$ be a partition of N into doubletons such that each agent in I_q prefers his doubleton's partner to any member of $I_{q+1} \cup \cdots \cup I_{n/2}$. To construct an initial status equilibrium, match each agent with his doubleton's partner and define a ranking P by iPj if i belongs to a weakly lower-indexed doubleton than j.
>
> (ii) In fact, the above pairing is the only initial status equilibrium pairing in a pair-rankable matching economy. This is because the two agents in I_1 must be matched in any initial status equilibrium since they top-rank each other and, for any equilibrium ranking, one of them can "afford" the other. The same argument then applies to the agents in I_2 and so on. Obviously, this pairing is also pairwise stable (see Alcalde (1994)).

> ### Example: The Common-ranking Two-sided Matching Economy
>
> The economy is uniquely pair-rankable with $I_q = \{i_q, j_q\}$. By Proposition 5.6, the unique initial status equilibrium is the pairing $\{i_1 \leftrightarrow j_1, i_2 \leftrightarrow j_2, \ldots\}$ with the status ranking P that ranks xPy if $x \in I_p$, $y \in I_q$ and $p \leq q$.

5.6 A Comparison of Approaches

The diagram summarizes the relationship between the different equilibrium concepts, pairwise stability (PS), and Pareto optimality (Pareto). The lines in the diagram depict weak inclusion. In particular, all equilibrium pairings are Pareto optimal (the First Welfare Theorem); only the Y-equilibrium satisfies the Second Welfare Theorem; and only the J2-, J3-, and Y-equilibrium are guaranteed to exist. The terms, status equilibrium (S) and initial status equilibrium (IS), are abbreviated.

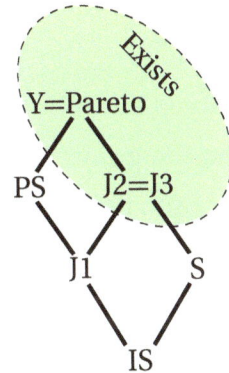

Figure 5.1 Relationship between the concepts.

5.7 The Majority Voting Economy

We now turn to compare our approach with that of Non-cooperative Game Theory. As mentioned, our battleground is the following *majority voting economy*: There is an odd number of agents ($n \geq 3$), each of whom chooses a position in $X = [-1, 1]$. Each agent i has continuous and strictly convex preferences over X with a unique peak, denoted by $peak^i$. All of the peaks are distinct and without loss of generality, we assume that $-1 < peak^1 < peak^2 < \cdots < peak^n < 1$. To simplify notation, denote the leftmost peak, the median peak, and the rightmost peak as L, M, and R, respectively. The set $F \subseteq X^N$ consists of all profiles for which at least $\tau = (n+1)/2$ members choose the same position. If a profile (x^i) has a point shared by at least τ members, we denote it by $O((x^i))$ and refer to it as the *overall position* (clearly, it is not possible to have two such positions).

The situation we have in mind is one where societal harmony requires that a majority of members declare the same position and if there is no such majority, then a crisis bursts. An example is a committee or a jury who, according to their procedure, must come out with a position that is supported by a majority of members. Another example is of a political party whose leaders must take positions on an issue. To prevent the public from becoming confused and abandoning the party, at least a majority of them need to take the same position.

Note that in Hotelling (1929) and its many extensions, an agent cares only about the group's position, while in Downs (1957), an agent also cares about his chosen position. We go a step further and assume that an agent cares only about his chosen position and does not care at all about the group's majority position.

5.8   Convex Y-equilibrium

First, we analyze the economy's *convex Y-equilibria* (Chapter 2). Recall that a convex Y-equilibrium is a configuration $\langle Y, (y^i) \rangle$ (where Y is a convex subset of X and (y^i) is a profile of choices from Y) that satisfies the three conditions:

(i)   Rationality: for all i, y^i is a $\succsim^i$-maximal position in Y.

(ii) Feasibility: $(y^i) \in F$.

(iii) Set maximality: there is no convex set $Z \supset Y$ and profile $(z^i) \in F$ such that z^i is a $\succsim^i$-maximal alternative in Z for all i.

Recall that, in any convex Y-equilibrium, the permissible set is closed (if not, then the closure of the permissible set with the same profile is a larger convex para-equilibrium). Since Y is convex and closed and all preference relations are strictly convex, every agent's maximal position is unique.

We now show that there are exactly two convex Y-equilibria in this economy and both have the overall position M (the median peak): a "rightist" equilibrium in which M and all positions to its right are permissible and a "leftist" equilibrium in which M and all positions to its left are permissible (see Figure 5.2).

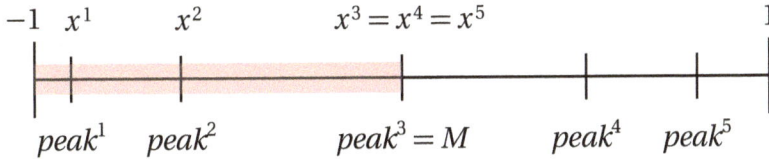

Figure 5.2 A leftist equilibrium

Proposition 5.7: Convex Y-equilibria in the Majority Voting Economy

In the majority voting economy, there are two convex Y-equilibria. Their permissible sets are $[-1, M]$ and $[M, 1]$. Both have the overall position M.

Proof:

The set $[-1, M]$ is a convex para-equilibrium permissible set because all of the rightist agents and the median voter vote M, thereby constituting a majority. Likewise, $[M, 1]$ is a convex para-equilibrium permissible set.

To show that $[-1, M]$ and $[M, 1]$ are convex Y-equilibrium permissible sets and that there are no others, it suffices to show that any convex para-equilibrium permissible set is a subset of either $[-1, M]$ or $[M, 1]$. To see this, note that if a convex permissible set contains points to both the left and right of M, then no position attracts majority support: M must be in the permissible set since it is convex and the median agent selects it, all leftist agents (a minority) choose positions to the left of M and all rightist agents (also a minority) choose positions to the right of M. Thus, every convex Y-para-equilibrium's permissible set is contained in $[-1, M]$ or $[M, 1]$.

At first glance, Proposition 5.7 appears to be a kind of "median voter theorem" since the only convex Y-equilibrium overall position is the median.

Thus, in terms of outcomes, the convex Y-equilibrium involves a compromise; however, the price of this "happy ending" is that only positions to one side of M are permitted.

5.9   Biased Preferences Equilibrium

To fit the model into Chapter 4's definition of an economy, we modify the specification of the agents' preferences as we did for the give-and-take economy. Assume that each agent i has two considerations in mind, labelled l and r, and maximizes the utility function $u^i(x) = u^i_l(x) + u^i_r(x)$ where u^i_l is strictly decreasing and represents an argument for leftist positions, while u^i_r is strictly increasing and represents an argument for rightist ones. The functions u^i_l and u^i_r are differentiable with non-zero and finite derivatives at each point. They are also strictly concave, which implies that their sum induces convex preferences with a unique peak, denoted by $peak^i$, and we assume that all peaks are different.

A bias (λ_l, λ_r) transforms an agent i's utility function into $\lambda_l u^i_l(x) + \lambda_r u^i_r(x)$. Consequently, a leftist bias (where $\lambda_l > \lambda_r$) moves the peak of every agent to the left, while a rightist bias (where $\lambda_l < \lambda_r$) moves all of the peaks to the right. There always exist extreme biased preferences equilibria where a majority of agents agree on the rightmost position supported by a rightist bias, which increases the weight of the rightist consideration strongly enough that at least a majority of individuals become extreme rightists. Likewise, there are also extreme leftist biased preferences equilibria.

It is possible that there are biased preferences equilibria where a majority of individuals move in one direction, and it just so happens that a majority of the biased peaks coincide but this would be a fluke occurrence. However, there is never a biased preferences equilibrium with a majority at the median position (since the peaks are distinct, a bias is necessary for agreement, but if there is a rightist bias, then any equilibrium must have a right-of-median overall position, and vice-versa if there is a leftist bias).

To summarize, extreme positions are always biased preferences equilibrium overall positions and the median never is, whereas the unique Y-equilibrium overall position is the median.

5.10 The Majority Voting Game and Nash Equilibrium

To model the majority voting economy $\langle N, X, (\succsim^i)_{i \in N}, F \rangle$ as a *strategic game*, let the set of players be N, and let each player's set of actions be the set of positions X. Each player j has a preference relation $\succsim_*^j$ on the set of all *choice profiles*, defined by $x = (x^i) \succsim_*^j y = (y^i)$ if either:

(i) $x \in F$ and $y \notin F$; or

(ii) both $x, y \in F$ or both $x, y \notin F$ and $x^j \succsim^j y^j$.

In other words, every agent's lexicographical first priority is harmony, and his second priority is his own position.

We apply the standard Nash equilibrium to this game. We distinguish between non-crisis Nash equilibria (in which a majority of players agree on a position) and crisis Nash equilibria (in which no overall position exists). Recall that n is odd. If $n > 3$, then there is a unique crisis equilibrium in which every agent chooses his own peak. No other crisis equilibria exist since, if the outcome of the game is a crisis, then every agent chooses his peak, because otherwise any agent could profitably deviate to his peak, whether or not that results in harmony. If $n = 3$, then a crisis equilibrium does not exist since any agent can deviate to one of the other two positions and thus, avoid a crisis.

In this game, the notion of a non-crisis Nash equilibrium is identical to that of the *social equilibrium* in Debreu (1952)'s model of generalized games (see Tóbiás (2022) for a review of conditions guaranteeing its existence). A social equilibrium is a profile of actions in F such that every player's action is a best response *from among the set of actions that are available to him given the other players' actions*. In other words, the profile after the deviation must be in F. Formally, $(x^i) \in F$ is a *social equilibrium* if for each i, the action x^i is optimal for i from among all the actions t^i such that $(t^i, x^{-i}) \in F$.

The difference between the Nash and Debreu formulations is purely semantic: every player is either not interested in moving from a non-crisis profile to a crisis profile (in the Nash formulation) or is not even allowed to do so (in Debreu's formulation).

All profiles in which a bare majority of exactly $\tau = (n+1)/2$ agents choose the same position (whatever it is), while the rest choose their peaks, are non-crisis Nash equilibria. These equilibria can be extremely unnatural in that the coalition which supports them does not have anything to do with the position being supported. In particular, there are non-crisis Nash equilibria for *any* overall position, even extreme ones that are outside of $[L, R]$, and the agents supporting the overall position need not be those whose peaks are closest to it. We will now see that there are no other non-crisis Nash equilibria.

> ### Proposition 5.8: Nash Equilibrium in the Voting Game
>
> If $n \geq 5$, then the set of non-crisis Nash equilibria in the voting game consists of all profiles for which there is a position chosen by exactly τ agents while the rest choose their peaks.

> ### Proof:
>
> These are Nash equilibria: No agent at the majority position can deviate profitably since, if he did so, then a crisis would ensue because his former position would no longer be a majority position and neither would his new position (all other agents are choosing their peaks which are distinct, so any new position would have at most two agents, but $n \geq 5$). All other agents are at their first-best, they choose their peak, and no crisis occurs. Therefore, they do not want to deviate.
>
> To see that there are no other non-crisis Nash equilibria, consider a Nash equilibrium in which at least τ agents choose a common position t. An agent who does not choose t is not critical in maintaining harmony and therefore, must be at his peak. If strictly more than τ agents choose t, then at least one of them is not at his peak and could deviate profitably.

Comment: In Richter and Rubinstein (2021), we conducted similar comparisons and reached similar conclusions regarding other conditions for "holding the group together":

(i) a consensus among a super majority of agents,

(ii) all positions are sufficiently close to the median position, or

(iii) all positions are sufficiently close to the average position.

5.11 Comparing our Approaches with Nash Equilibrium

The above analysis clarifies the significant differences between the convex Y-equilibrium, the biased preferences equilibrium, and the Nash equilibrium of the above political game. For the convex Y-equilibrium concept, M is the only overall position. For the biased preferences equilibrium concept, typically only the extreme positions, -1 and 1, are overall positions. In contrast, for the Nash equilibrium concept, all positions, even those outside the range $[L, R]$, are overall positions. Furthermore, a convex Y-equilibrium is "monotonic" in the sense that if agent i's ideal position is to the left of j's then his chosen position is weakly to the left of j's. In contrast, there are *always* non-monotonic Nash equilibria. The biased preferences equilibrium case is less clear: the existence of a non-monotonic equilibrium depends on the underlying utility functions.

Notice that the Nash equilibria require a high degree of coordination between the agents. In contrast, the Y-equilibrium and biased preferences equilibrium concepts only require that agents know either the social restrictions or biases, but not the behaviour of others. This is like the marketplace where individuals only need to know prices, but not other agents' actions.

Let us emphasise: we are not saying that the standard game-theoretical approach is "wrong", nor do we insist that the Y-equilibrium or biased preferences equilibrium approaches are "right". Rather, and as already mentioned, we are suggesting that the reader not automatically apply Nash-equilibrium-like concepts but instead considers alternative solution concepts in the spirit of those described in this book.

References

Abdulkadıroğlu, Atıla, and Tayfun Sönmez (1998), "Random serial dictatorship and the core from random endowments in house allocation problems." *Econometrica*, 66, 689–701. [18]

Alcalde, José (1994), "Exchange-proofness or divorce-proofness? Stability in one-sided matching markets." *Economic Design*, 1, 275–287. [126]

Atakan, Alp, Michael Richter, and Matan Tsur (2023), "Efficient search, matching, investments." *mimeo.* [108]

Bagwell, Kyle (2007), "The economic analysis of advertising." *Handbook of Industrial Organization*, 3, 1701–1844. [92]

Balasko, Yves (1979), "Budget-constrained Pareto-efficient allocations." *Journal of Economic Theory*, 21, 359–379. [101]

Becker, Gary S., and Kevin M. Murphy (1988), "A theory of rational addiction." *Journal of Political Economy*, 96, 675–700. [92]

Benassy, Jean-Pascal (1986), *Macroeconomics: An Introduction to the Non-Walrasian Approach*. Elsevier, New York, NY. [100]

Birkhoff, Garrett (1946), "Tres observaciones sobre el algebra lineal (three observations on linear algebra)." *Universidad Nacional de Tucumán Revista Serie A*, 5, 147–151. [109]

Bowles, Samuel, and Herbert Gintis (1992), "Power and wealth in a competitive capitalist economy." *Philosophy and Public Affairs*, 21, 324–353. [13]

Buchanan, James M. (1965), "An economic theory of clubs." *Economica*, 32, 1–14. [6]

Budish, Eric, Yeon-Koo Che, Fuhito Kojima, and Paul Milgrom (2013), "Designing random allocation mechanisms: Theory and applications." *American Economic Review*, 103, 585–623. [109]

Debreu, Gerard (1952), "A social equilibrium existence theorem." *Proceedings of the National Academy of Sciences*, 38, 886 – 893. [131]

Downs, Anthony (1957), *An Economic Theory of Democracy*. Harper. [128]

Edelman, Paul H., and Robert E. Jamison (1985), "The theory of convex geometries." *Geometriae Dedicata*, 19, 247–270. [72]

Edgeworth, Francis Ysidro (1881), *Mathematical Psychics: An Essay on the Application of Mathematics to the Moral Sciences*, volume 10. CK Paul. [5]

Foley, Duncan Karl (1966), *Resource allocation and the public sector*. Yale University. [43, 55]

Gale, David (1984), "Equilibrium in a discrete exchange economy with money." *International Journal of Game Theory*, 13, 61–64. [105]

Gale, David, and Lloyd S. Shapley (1962), "College admissions and the stability of marriage." *The American Mathematical Monthly*, 69, 9–15. [27, 111, 113]

Gale, David, and Marilda Sotomayor (1985), "Some remarks on the stable matching problem." *Discrete Applied Mathematics*, 11, 223–232. [27]

Gibbs, Laura (2002), *Aesop's Fables*. Oxford World's Classics, Oxford University Press. [91]

Grossman, Herschel I. (1995), "Robin hood and the redistribution of property income." *European Journal of Political Economy*, 11, 399–410. [13]

Hirshleifer, Jack (1994), "The dark side of the force: Western economic association international 1993 presidential address." *Economic Inquiry*, 32, 1–10. [13]

Hotelling, Harold (1929), "Stability in competition." *The Economic Journal*, 39, 41–57. [128]

Keiding, Hans (1981), "Existence of budget constrained Pareto efficient allocations." *Journal of Economic Theory*, 24, 393–397. [101]

Malinvaud, Edmond (1972), *Lectures on Microeconomic Theory*. Advanced textbooks in economics, North-Holland Publishing Company. [47]

Osborne, Martin, and Ariel Rubinstein (2023), *Models in Microeconomic Theory*, Expanded second edition. Open Book Publishers. [23]

Piccione, Michele, and Ariel Rubinstein (2007), "Equilibrium in the jungle." *The Economic Journal*, 117, 883–896. [14, 33, 34]

Richter, Michael, and Ariel Rubinstein (2015), "Back to fundamentals: Equilibrium in abstract economies." *American Economic Review*, 105, 2570–94. [65, 82]

Richter, Michael, and Ariel Rubinstein (2019), "Convex preferences: A new definition." *Theoretical Economics*, 14, 1169–1183. [71, 72, 75, 84]

Richter, Michael, and Ariel Rubinstein (2020), "The permissible and the forbidden." *Journal of Economic Theory*, 188, 105042. [38, 61]

Richter, Michael, and Ariel Rubinstein (2021), "Holding a group together: Non-game theory versus game theory." *The Economic Journal*, 131, 2629–2641. [112, 133]

Richter, Michael, and Ariel Rubinstein (2024), "Unilateral stability in matching problems." *Journal of Economic Theory*, 216, 105780. [111, 122, 124]

Rubinstein, Ariel (2005), *Lecture Notes in Microeconomic Theory*. Princeton, NJ: Princeton University. [46]

Rubinstein, Ariel (2012), *Economic Fables*. Open Book Publishers. [1]

Rubinstein, Ariel, and Asher Wolinksy (2022), "Biased preferences equilibrium." *Economics and Philosophy*, 38, 24–33. [91]

Rubinstein, Ariel, and Kemal Yıldız (2022), "An étude in modeling the definability of equilibrium." *Review of Economic Design*, 26, 543–552. [27, 115]

Shapley, Lloyd, and Herbert Scarf (1974), "On cores and indivisibility." *Journal of Mathematical Economics*, 1, 23–37. [5, 14, 21, 22, 69, 88, 104]

Shapley, Lloyd S., and Martin Shubik (1971), "The assignment game I: The core." *International Journal of Game Theory*, 1, 111–130. [105, 106, 107, 108]

Sprumont, Yves (1991), "The division problem with single-peaked preferences: A characterization of the uniform allocation rule." *Econometrica*, 59, 509–519. [6]

Tóbiás, Áron (2022), "Equilibrium non-existence in generalized games." *Games and Economic Behavior*, 135, 327–337. [131]

Varian, Hal (1974), "Equity, envy, and efficiency." *Journal of Economic Theory*, 9, 63–91. [43, 55]

About the Team

Alessandra Tosi was the managing editor for this book.

Jennifer Moriarty copyedited the book.

The cover image was created by Ariel Rubinstein from a concept by Michael Richter and Ariel Rubinstein. The cover of this book was produced by Jeevanjot Kaur Nagpal in InDesign using Fontin and Calibri fonts.

Michael Richter and Ariel Rubinstein typeset the book in LaTeX and produced the paperback and hardback editions.

Cameron Craig produced the PDF and HTML editions. Conversion was performed with open source software freely available on our GitHub page at https://github.com/OpenBookPublishers.

This book need not end here...

Share

All our books — including the one you have just read — are free to access online so that students, researchers and members of the public who can't afford a printed edition will have access to the same ideas. This title will be accessed online by hundreds of readers each month across the globe: why not share the link so that someone you know is one of them?

This book and additional content is available at:
https://doi.org/10.11647/OBP.0404

Donate

Open Book Publishers is an award-winning, scholar-led, not-for-profit press making knowledge freely available one book at a time. We don't charge authors to publish with us: instead, our work is supported by our library members and by donations from people who believe that research shouldn't be locked behind paywalls.

Why not join them in freeing knowledge by supporting us:
https://www.openbookpublishers.com/support-us

Follow @OpenBookPublish

Read more at the Open Book Publishers **BLOG**

You may also be interested in:

Models in Microeconomic Theory
Expanded Second Edition

Martin J. Osborne and Ariel Rubinstein

https://doi.org/10.11647/obp.0361

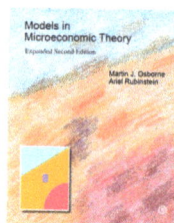

Economic Fables

Ariel Rubinstein

https://doi.org/10.11647/obp.0020

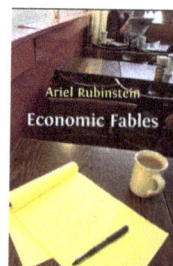

Is Behavioral Economics Doomed?
The Ordinary versus the Extraordinary

David K. Levine

https://doi.org/10.11647/obp.0021

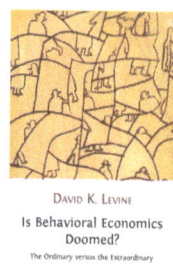

www.ingramcontent.com/pod-product-compliance
Lightning Source LLC
Chambersburg PA
CBHW050039220326
41599CB00041B/7215